THE MORNING EDITION

by

Andrew Lafleche

Books by

ANDREW LAFLECHE

Ashes

No Diplomacy

Shameless

A Pardonable Offence

One Hundred Little Victories

On Writing

Merica, Merica on the Wall

After I Turn into Alcohol

Eyes Wide

Ride

Grateful acknowledgment is given to the following publications where some of these stories originally appeared: Commuter Lit, Metonym Literary Journal, Merrimack Review, Route 7 Review, Phenomenal Literature, The Fictional Cafe, Lalitamba, Haunted MTL, In Parenthesis and Scarlet Leaf Review.

Contents

Full Disclosure

"Full disclosure," Johnny said to the lady. She sat adjacent to him, cross-legged, wearing a blue blouse, and stared at her legal pad. A glass of water perspired on the table beside her. The light from the afternoon sun shone through the window behind. "If I'm being completely honest, every night before I go to bed I pray–not really pray–I wish, I wonder, I lust that before I wake, I die. Every day. And every morning, I wake up disappointed."

The lady looked at him. Her eyes betrayed that she might have to report this.

"I mean," Johnny said. "I can't really say this stuff to anybody out there, and if I can't say it here, then how are we supposed to accomplish anything?" Despite having never told anyone this before he knew he had to diffuse the situation before he found himself committed.

He imagined how she might excuse herself and give a signal to the receptionist or to another therapist in the office who would then call the police. She'd return and continue the session as if nothing sinister was at play. In the time it took for him to finish his final thought and before the lady could respond he would hear a knock at the door and the police would be entering before having been invited into the room. Handcuffs around his wrists he'd be taken against his will to wherever, drugged, and locked away until they deemed him no longer a threat to society or himself. Johnny regretted admitting his secret. He should have never come here to begin with. He stared out the window. A bird flew by and landed on the grassy knoll below. It was only the second floor.

"Will you excuse me a moment?" the lady asked.

Johnny smiled.

Kenmore Square

The breeze was colder than expected for the beginning of May. Tulips had been in full bloom for nearly a month. The rains had come and gone. The breeze this morning belonged to one of late fall. Still, the newspaper pressed against the glass of the rack reported the month of May. Luke zipped his sweater tighter and checked his watch. Seven-thirty. The bus would be there soon. A man approached, accompanied by a small child. When they neared Luke, they stopped and leaned against the red brick bus station wall.

"Do you really think we'll make it before dinner?" the boy asked, his eyes full of hope.

"You bet," the man said. "We might even get there in time to walk down to Kenmore Square."

"What's Kenmore Square?"

"A place where a whole bunch of streets meet."

"The streets meet in a square?"

"Right underneath the giant Citgo sign."

"What's a Citgo sign?" the boy asked.

"The landmark of Kenmore Square."

The boy pondered this. He tilted his head and rested his fist on his chin. "A sign is the landmark of Kenmore Square?"

"Not just a sign, the sign," the man said. "And you've already seen it."

"I have?"

"Every time they hit a home run over left field, the cameras pick it up."

"I don't think I've seen it before."

"The white sign with the glowing heart."

"Oh," the boy said. "I've seen that sign."

"I know you have."

"Not in real life, though. Do you think we'll make it in time to go down to Kenmore Square and see the sign?"

"The Citgo sign," the man said. "And I think we might."

"Where is it?"

"The sign?"

"Yeah."

"It's on top of Barnes & Noble."

"Why is the Citgo sign on top of the Barnes & Noble bookstore?"

"It was a Citgo office before it was the bookstore."

"Hmm," the boy said. He pressed a finger to his temple and rested his thumb on his chin. "I hope we get there in time to see the sign."

The breeze kicked up leaves from the gutter. They appeared suspended before returning to the pavement. The young boy tightened his scarf and pulled his hat lower.

#

The bus arrived ten minutes late. The man, the boy, and Luke were the only passengers to board at this stop.

"Heading to Boston?" the driver asked.

"Sure are," the boy said. "We're going to see the Red Sox, and if we're there early enough we might even go down to the square and see the Citgo."

"We're going to pass straight through Kenmore Square," the driver said. "You'll be able to see the sign right from your seat."

"Really?" the boy asked.

The driver nodded.

"Still," the boy said. "I think I'd like to see it in real life, from the street."

The driver grinned. The man and the boy chose seats together.

"Boston?" the driver asked Luke.

Luke nodded and took a window seat near the man and young boy.

The bus station disappeared into the city. Luke relaxed into the worn upholstery. He unzipped his jacket and exhaled deeply. It had been a long winter. "At the end of a long year," he said. He scanned the seats nearby. Nobody looked as if they had heard him. Luke was relieved.

Boston will be different, he assured himself, eyes closed.

#

"What if we don't make it in time?" the boy asked.

"We'll make it in time," the man said.

"For Kenmore Square?"

"For the ballgame."

"I meant for Kenmore Square," the boy said.

"We'll definitely make the ballgame. That's what we're going for, remember?"

"But now that I know about the square and the sign, I really want to go there too," the boy said.

"We'll try our best."

"I think we'll make it for both."

The man nodded. "I hope so."

#

Luke wondered when the last time he spoke to his father was. He remembered when he was a boy how his dad would take him to ball games whenever he had a Saturday off work. How they would ride the bus together to the stadium and get hot dogs with mustard from the stand outside before going in. During the seventh-inning stretch, his dad would take him for a bag of peanuts and a Coca-Cola and buy himself a single can of Samuel Adams. Mom never allowed soda or beer in the house. The Saturday ball game was a father and son pact, protected by the secret they shared.

Luke looked over to the man and young boy. The boy had stopped talking and was resting against the arm of the man. He looked asleep, but Luke couldn't be sure.

The man caught Luke's gaze and pursed his eye's quizzically.

"Sorry," Luke said. "I was just remembering how me and my dad would take the bus to the game when I was the boy's age."

"It's important," the man said. He lifted his arm gently, so not to disturb the young boy, and rested it over the boy's shoulder. "Me and my dad went once a month till the year he died."

Luke nodded. "Enjoy your day."

"We will," the man said.

#

"Kenmore Square," the driver hollered.

The boy jumped up in his seat. "We're here?"

"We made it," the man said. "Look. You can see the sign right up there."

The boy leaned over the man and looked up out the window.

Luke leaned over and looked out as well.

"Wow," the boy said. "It's bigger than it looks on TV."

"It's even bigger when you're standing under it," the man said.

"Are we going to get to stand under it?"

"I think we have just enough time."

The boy beamed and then stopped. He looked as if he were about to cry.

"What's the matter?" the man asked.

"Do you think Mom would have liked the Citgo sign?"

The man bowed his head. "It's where we first met."

The boy hung his head. "I really miss her."

"Me too," the man said. He kissed the top of the boy's head. "Every day."

The Eagle

Laura sat beneath the near bare birch tree. She sat beneath the tree and stewed. Across the yard, the boys were carrying-on in their tree fort. The tree fort dad had built for Alex the previous summer. The tree fort which explicitly expressed in bright red spray paint, No Girls Aloud.

Laura kicked at the leaves she'd raked into a pile. "It's *allowed*, stupid," she cursed.

Of course, stupid wasn't really a curse word, but if mother ever heard her use it, Laura would have earned a smack. Girls do not use words like *stupid.* And they don't spit.

Laura growled her throat, sucked all her saliva onto the base of her tongue, and hawked a loogie.

The slimy string hung from her lip and threatened to soak her flannel button-down. She huffed. "Girls don't spit," she whined, wiping the failed spittle from her chin. "Girls don't swear. Girls don't play in the mud. Girl's can't go in the tree fort. Girls can't, can't, can't."

She pressed her back into the sturdy tree trunk and glared at the tree fort. The leaves on the maple were orange. Orange is ugly on trees, which is why birch trees always look prettier than maple trees in the fall. Their leaves only turn yellow before descending to the ground. Green and yellow are palatable. Orange and green, however, should never be seen *except for in the washing machine.*

Laura's mother's voice, again. Laura's mother's voice, always.

She looked up. Above the reaching branches, the grey clouds threatened snow. But that's it. Halloween would come first—then the snow.

An eagle soared into view, wings still, effortless. Before Laura could completely appreciate the majestic creature, six little birds darted toward it. Their violent wings, if not in the sky and instead were flapping on the surface of a lake, would have looked like drowning.

The eagle glanced at its aggressors, pressed gently into the air beneath its extended wings, and gracefully ascended higher, annoyed or saddened, it was hard to tell from where Laura sat.

"Stupid birds, stupid boys, stupid mom. Girls can't go in the tree fort because girls don't climb trees." Laura punched the ground, not hard, but enough to show that she meant business. "I can climb trees."

The lowest branch towered one jump out of reach. Laura stared at it, focused, bent her knees and jumped with all her might.

To her surprise, her hands reached past the branch. She could have kissed the crisp whiteness she jumped so high. Quickly, she reached an arm around and clung to the branch. Laura swung her hips and managed to get a foot over the crux. She wiggled, and pulled, and grunted, and groaned, and in the struggle righted herself on the lowest branch, base camp for her climb.

"I don't need your stupid tree or your fort!" She yelled across the yard.

The boy's carrying-on quieted. Alex peaked out the curtain-clad window.

Mac's head popped out beside his.

"Laura," Alex whined. He was at the age where no matter how serious he wanted to sound, his voice was always the octave of whining. "Laura," he whined again, "get down from there before you hurt yourself."

Laura stuck out her tongue, a twelve-year-old's middle finger.

"I'm telling mom," Alex said, whining.

A few feet away hung another sturdy limp. She bounded for it.

Branch by branch she scaled the tree until she was as high as the boys were.

"You're too high, Laura," Alex said, concerned, but still whiny.

Laura grinned. "You're just jeal-ous," she called in a sing-song voice.

Alex started again, but it was no use. Laura had continued her climb and by all appearances, didn't look like she was going to stop until she reached the top.

The boys hurried down the ladder. From the ground, Laura almost couldn't be seen she was so high. Laura was higher than the house.

"Laura! You come down, right now!" Alex demanded.

The patio door slid open. Alex and Laura's mother's head poked through the opening.

"What's going on out here?" she barked. "You're terrorizing the whole neighbourhood with your yelling." She looked to the pile of leaves where Laura had been raking. Obviously, Laura wasn't there.

Alex was about to explain everything when Laura called from her perch at the top of the tree.

"I thought you said girls couldn't climb trees!" She yelled down, gloating.

Alex added, "I tried to get her to stop but she—"

"Laura Jessica Parker!" her mother yelled. "You come down from there right now."

Laura rolled her eyes. She mouthed *you come down from there right now.*

"I can see you sticking out your tongue, young lady!"

Laura sighed.

She looked around. She looked down. Her mother and brother and Mac looked ridiculous, miniature, yelling up at her. They looked fake, like she was in the rafters looking down at the characters and the set of a school play. The backyard looked smaller. The roof looked flat. Everything that seemed so big from below, now looked remarkably dull.

"If you don't come down from there this instant—" her mother yelled, but it was too late.

Laura let go what was left of the trunk at the top of the tree. She bent her knees and lunged off the branch into the air, into nothing.

The three miniatures screamed Laura's name.

Laura, smiling, extended her arms. She understood the eagle.

Madam Brady's

Soon after the mamma left the room, three open palm whacks struck the front door. The boy jumped.

"Judge Randy," the boy's mamma said. "Good evening, Sir."

The Judge removed his hat and stepped inside. "Ms. Brady."

She extended an arm for him to drape his coat over. "Can I get you a drink while we wait for the others?"

"Two fingers of scotch, please."

"You just head down to the lounge and make yourself comfortable."

"You're an impeccable hostess, Ms. Brady."

"I don't imagine you'd be here all these years if I weren't."

The lounge wasn't a lounge, unless a dimly lit space soon to be filled with cigar smoke and serious gambling made it one. No. This was Ms. Brady's gig alright, an underground casino of sorts, and calling it a lounge sounded better than calling it a basement; only a lounge allowed everybody to feel dignified.

Green lampshades hung from the ceiling. On the far side of the room, across from the stairs, stood a hand carved wooden bar, it's leather counter sunk with five holes for drinks. On nights where the town's elite had not reserved Ms. Brady's private service, she dealt blackjack from behind the counter while Texas hold 'em players policed their own game at the main table. Solitary plush cushioned chairs were paired with wooden tables around the room where gamblers could become momentary spectators as they sought refuge from their losses but weren't quite ready to quit.

Judge Randy assumed his position third seat from the dealer. For as long as he'd been visiting Ms. Brady's he always sat in the same seat, each time winning as much as he lost, not including the bills he occasionally dropped when he pulled in a winning pot and stuffed the paper in his pockets.

Even if the little boy hadn't heard his mamma greet Judge Randy, he would have known who it was by the way the Judge dropped into his seat as if he had no fear the chair wouldn't hold his Texan figure. Furthermore, the Judge always wore low-cut leather cowboy boots, brown, no matter what colour pants he was wearing.

The boy minded his posture, hidden beneath the table, now that the guests had started to arrive, heeding his mother's warning not to touch anyone, or to make a sound.

Ms. Brady looked like royalty as she descended the stairs, purple dress topped with large gold earrings.

"Your scotch, Judge," Ms. Brady said.

The Judge sipped his drink.

"Can I get you anything else?"

"Just an ashtray, dear."

She removed a stack of ashtrays from behind the blackjack table and placed one in front of the Judge. She set the rest at the other seats. Ms. Brady struck a match and held it to Judge Randy's cigar. He puffed three quick puffs and it was lit.

Three whacks at the door. The boy gasped. If Ms. Brady heard, she didn't flinch. "Excuse me, Judge," Ms. Brady said. The Judge waved his hand. Ms. Brady dipped her head and disappeared upstairs.

"Boy," the Judge said. He lifted the table skirt.

"Sir," the boy responded, knowing if his mamma ever caught him making a peep, he would get a lashing that would keep him from sitting for a week.

"You stay away from that Dr. Baxter when he shows up, no matter how big the bill he waves at you," the Judge said. "You understand me, boy?"

"Sir," the boy said, not quite sure why Judge Randy disliked Dr. Baxter so sincerely.

The Judge pulled a fifty-dollar bill from his fold and passed it to the boy. "You keep this," he said. "It's yours. Don't give it to your mamma, don't tell nobody I gave it to you. It's just for you. Maybe one day you'll be able to escape this place."

"Thank you, sir," the boy said.

"If that Dr. Baxter ever even looks at you with his queer eyes, you tell me, okay boy?"

"Sir," the boy said. He wondered what the Judge meant by queer eyes.

The Judge let the skirt fall to conceal the young boy in his place.

"Lady Madam," Harold Coffee said, greeting Ms. Brady.

Dr. Baxter grinned.

Ms. Brady fought the chill which ran her spine.

"I'll bring your drinks down right away," she said.

The two men hung their jackets and made their way downstairs.

Ms. Brady poured the drinks. She paused at the top of the stairs to compose herself when the third knock came. Her shoulders tensed.

Ms. Brady set the two drinks on the ledge and straightened herself. She forced a smile and answered the door.

Mr. Lapointe towered at six and a half feet. He tipped his hat to Ms. Brady as she welcomed him into her home. "Ma'am," Mr. Lapointe said.

Ms. Brady closed the door behind him. "Jimmy," she said and locked the deadbolt behind him. "Ma'am is my mother's name. I'll have none of that in this house."

Mr. Lapointe smiled. "Lady Brady."

Ms. Brady smiled, "Whisky and ale?"

"You're a real gem, don't matter what anybody says," Mr. Lapointe said.

Ms. Brady pretended to be offended, mouth agape. Mr. Lapointe leaned in and kissed her cheek.

"It's good to see you again, Jimmy."

Once all the men were seated, Ms. Brady started. "Let's have a good clean game."

"How clean do you expect tonight to be?" the Judge quipped. "You mustn't have heard about Coffee's ruthless double-ender he fleeced poor old Ms. Schrodinger into with her real estate down by the river."

"Ruthless?" Harold Coffee said with a grin. "You make me sound like a gangster!"

Both men were good friends and had been for a long time. "I had nothing but Ms. Schrodinger's best interest at heart that entire transaction."

The Judge snickered. "'Course you did."

"If you want to talk ruthless, how about this guy and his nine percent loans he's marketing as a deal."

Jimmy set his whisky on the table. "I can remember mortgage rates hovering around twenty-four points," he said. "I'd take 9% any day."

Ms. Brady placed Mr. Lapointe's glass in the holder.

"I'm with Jimmy," Dr. Baxter said. "Nine percent is a steal. Everybody has to make a living, don't they?"

Ms. Brady knew if she let the men continue jabbing, they would go on for an hour without a card played. "Five-Card-Stud to start?"

The men agreed.

"Alright," she said. "No blinds. Four rounds of betting. All five of your cards must be played in the showdown."

Mr. Lapointe turned to the Judge and said, "You might find this interesting."

The Judge raised the bet. "Shoot."

"Ms. Stacy was in the bank the other day, and I was asking her how she was making out with Jerry having passed and all; her two boys–"

"Yes, a terrible tragedy," Dr. Baxter interrupted. "If a doc tells you to have your colon checked, take the finger."

"She actually mentioned you, Baxter," Mr. Lapointe said.

The Judge glared at Dr. Baxter.

"She did, did she?" Dr. Baxter said. "What a fine woman."

"She said you offered pro-Bono dental work for Oscar and Aaron."

"That's mighty generous of you," Harold Coffee said.

"It really is the least I could do," Dr. Baxter said. "Jerry was a friend of mine, his family's been long time clients of my practice. If the situation were reversed, I'm sure he would have done the same." He pulled on his drink, smiled. "Anything I can do to help."

"I'm sure," the Judge said. His distaste for Dr. Baxter was public knowledge.

"I wasn't referring to your pro-Bono work, Baxter," Mr. Lapointe continued. "Ms. Stacy said you offered Oscar a job minding your lawn over the summer."

"Oh, that's right," Dr. Baxter said. "Figured the boy could use some extra cash, keep him out of trouble, you know, without his father around to keep him in line."

The Judge's face hardened.

"Whatever happened to the Harris boy?" Mr. Lapointe asked.

A rabid flicker flashed across Dr. Baxter's face and disappeared. "Moved out east to live with his dad," he said.

"You and him were pretty friendly," Mr. Lapointe added.

It was dare, a line drawn in the sand, naming something not to be named.

"It seems I remember a night back in university," Harold Coffee said. "Where a frat woke up after a party claiming–"

"Gentlemen," Ms. Brady interrupted. "Are all bets in?"

The men stared at their hands.

Harold Coffee turned his empty drink. "Could I trouble you for another gin and tonic?"

"Aye," Mr. Lapointe said. "And another sipper and ale, if you wouldn't mind."

Dr. Baxter said, "Another round for me too, please."

The Judge didn't say a word; he nodded.

The conversation remained muted while Ms. Brady refreshed the drinks upstairs. If she didn't intervene every now and again, the game would disperse early. She needed the money.

When Ms. Brady returned, Harold Coffee said to the Judge, "The rumour mill has it you're thinking about running in the primaries."

The Judge smiled. "You know I don't comment on rumours."

"Blink twice if it's true," Harold Coffee said.

"Harold," the Judge laughed. "I'm two years from retirement. Do you really think I want to be locked away in an office, pushing paper for some Congressman's agenda?"

Ms. Brady placed new glasses in front each of the men and assumed her position at the head of the table. "Shall we continue?"

The Morning Edition

It was very early when the man woke beneath the tree he had rested against the night before. His clothes were damp with the morning dew. His lips, stained purple by wine, were crusty. In the distance, a car braked and the weighted thud of a newspaper stack struck the sidewalk. The man righted himself against the tree then rubbed the sleep from his burning eyes. He looked at his crotch and was relieved he hadn't pissed himself. A pair of joggers passed and muttered, "Fucking drunk." The man stood, sighed, and thought maybe today he wouldn't drink. On his walk home he assured himself he would not drink today.

"You said this was the last time, last time," Sally said, when he opened the door.

"I'm trying," he said, and meant it.

"Where were you last night?"

"I worked the late shift."

"And then?"

"I stopped by Murphy's on the way home."

"Of course you did."

"A man can't put in his eight hours and relax with a beer afterwards?"

"When have you ever had 'a beer'?"

"This is how you want to start the day? I said I was sorry."

"Start the day? Do you think I can sleep when you're out all night, drunk off your ass, fucking who knows who?"

"Don't star–"

"And no, you didn't apologize."

The couple stared at each other.

Beads of sweat formed on the man's forehead. Barley seeped through his pores. Whisky soured his breath. He decided not to argue. "I'm going upstairs to shower."

Even with the door closed, he could hear his wife crying in the kitchen. He turned on the water, hot, and let it run. Steam filled the bathroom. He couldn't hear his wife any longer. The man inhaled deep like a good pull from a cigarette. He closed his eyes and exhaled the air. "I was just a little drunk," he said to himself. "She always thinks it's something else. It was just a drunk."

The man was slow to shower, slow to shave, slow to dress, and even when presentable, lingered at the top of the stairs. He wasn't hung over; long ago he learned that a hot shower and a clean shave subdued any strong aftereffect. He listened for his wife. She was on the phone but he didn't know with whom.

"Yeah," Sally said. "This morning."

The man hardened his face. There had been a time when marital issues were dealt with at home.

"You should have seen him. The bags under his eyes like he'd been up all night doing cocaine, nose red, teeth stained Merlot. I'm sick even thinking about it."

The man chuckled. It wasn't that bad. And now, cleaned up, no one could even tell.

"I'm doing it," Sally said. She sounded confident.

The man started down the stairs.

"For sure this time."

His wife was sitting at the kitchen table. She wasn't crying any more. A stoic resolve had become her face. "I'll call you later."

He poured himself a coffee, "Who was that?"

"Excuse me?" Sally said.

"On the phone."

The man's wife stared at her coffee.

"Sally," the man said. He paused. He wanted her to look up at him. When she did, he said, "I'm sorry."

The wife laughed.

"This is a joke now?" the man said.

"It has to be," Sally said. "Who are we kidding?"

"What?"

"You and me. Our marriage. This."

He sat in the chair across from her. "Things aren't so bad."

"You didn't come home last night."

"It was a mistake," he said. "But nothing happened. I promise."

"Wow," she said. "You promise. Doesn't that sound ridiculous to you?"

"You accused me of cheating."

"It wouldn't be the first time," said Sally. Her glare taunted.

The man set down his mug. He tried to keep his fists from clenching. "That was a long time ago," he said. "Before we were married."

"And that makes it all right? I'm such an idiot."

"I got off work then I stopped by Murphy's and had a couple drinks."

"You said 'a beer.'"

"It was a long day Sally. I was exhausted and didn't realize it until I was falling asleep."

"Why didn't you call?"

"I'm trying, for real. I knew you'd be disappointed that I stopped for a drink, I didn't want you to be upset."

"How's that working out for you?"

The man pressed his face into his hands.

"Where did you sleep last night?"

"Who were you talking to?" he said.

"Not until you answer my question."

"I fell asleep in the park."

"The park?"

"When I left the bar, I stopped to rest a minute and must have closed my eyes."

"You passed out in the park? Like a bum?"

"Please, I already got it from two joggers this morning."

"People saw you?"

"Would you rather I drove?"

"I'd rather I didn't have a drunk for a husband."

"Who were you talking to?"

The wife stood up, placed her mug in the sink, and leaned against the counter. She crossed her arms. "I was talking to my mother."

"Your mother?"

Sally averted her eyes.

"Why would you involve her? Why not come to me? Do you know what this does to our relationship?"

"What relationship? I never see you. You're always at work, or at the bar, or out with whoev–"

"I'm not having an affair. You need to stop that."

"Don't tell me what to do."

"You can't pit your mother against me."

"You've done that all on your own."

"I have done nothing."

"When was the last time we had sex?"

"You're always asleep when I get home."

"Because you don't come home until late. And when you are home, you're half cut on rye and ginger."

"You knew I enjoyed my drink before we got married."

"You love the bottle more than you love me."

"That's not true." The man stood up, walked over to his wife and placed his hands on her hips. He traced the small of her back to her shoulders. He rested his forehead on hers and said, "I love you, Sally. I do. More than anything." He tried to kiss her.

"Gross," she pushed him away. "I can smell the booze on your breath. Did you even brush your teeth?"

The man slammed his hand on the counter. "Goddammit Sally!"

"You did this," she said. "You did it. Not me."

"It was an accident."

"How many more accidents before you come home at night?"

"What do you want me to say?"

"I want a divorce."

"What?"

"I. Want. A. Divorce."

"Did your mother put you up to this?"

"My mother had nothing to do with this."

"She didn't?"

"Don't patronize me."

"We're not getting a divorce."

"Well I don't want to be your wife anymore."

"It won't happen again."

"You're damn right it won't."

The man's face turned red. His body tensed. He raised his hand.

"Look at you now," she said. She shook her head. "I'll being staying at mother's until you can move your things out."

"Sally, I didn't mean that," the man said. "You know I'd never hit you."

The man's wife looked him straight in the eyes. Her eyes were wet. "I don't think I do," she said, and stepped past him. "Please don't take long. It will be better for both of us." She closed the door behind her without saying goodbye.

The man steadied himself on the counter. Things couldn't be that bad, he thought. Or, how hadn't he noticed? He rinsed the mug then knelt to open the cupboard. He removed the window cleaner, the bleach, the scrub pads, and the bucket. In the back corner, hidden safe where he left it, was a tall pebbled bottle, corked at the mouth. The sight of the amber liquid calmed his screaming nerves. He removed the bottle and poured himself two fingers. Today might have been the day he didn't drink, he thought, tossing back the whisky. It sure could have been, he reasoned, and poured another glass.

The Life and Death of Arthur Miller

Fourteen days after Arthur Miller's sixteenth birthday, both his parents were killed in an automobile accident when a drunken driver swerved into their lane as they returned home from a night at the theatre. Their deaths occurred instantly, and to that effect, neither were able to be presented with an open coffin at their post-life nuptials. The last time Arthur saw his parents alive was in the moments following Sunday dinner, his mother in a dress, glowing, his father dressed handsomely, saying, "When you finally meet the woman who makes the world stand still, son, don't ever quit doing for her what you did at the start. That way there will never be an end."

Arthur clung to these words in the weeks that followed. He clung to everything his father said, for his father was the wisest person Arthur had ever known. The only compromise Arthur made against what he knew his father wouldn't approve, was that immediately following the funeral, Arthur dropped out of school—postponed his education was the rationalization—to take up work at the local textile mill in order to afford residence in the house his parents had raised him in; to cover the cost of the burial; to pay for all the costs of living he never knew as a child, for his father had always provided. There was the phone bill, but only solicitors ever called. The electric company had to be paid, the town for taxes, the oil for the furnace, groceries; and the occasional article of clothing. The expenses were not great, he was alone after all, but as any sixteen-year-old forced to earn his way in the world can attest, it was not easy.

After several months, more so a year, Arthur settled into his new normal, rising with the sun during the summer months, before the sun in winter, grab his lunch pail which he prepared the evening prior, and walked to his post at the mill. In the summer, he finished in time to observe the sun set as he walked home to prepare his lunch for the following day. In the winter, it was dark as when he left for work in the morning. Day in, day out, Arthur became accustomed to the grind of existence.

In time, he was able to save enough money to purchase his first vehicle, a practical blue Chevrolet Caprice Classic, and taught himself to drive. Outsiders thought his choice morbid, as it was the same model car his parents had been killed in, but Arthur didn't think so. He found two rubber bands and secured a picture of his parents to the visor above the driver's seat. Every time he sat behind the steering wheel, he was reminded to treat the privilege of driving most seriously. And he did. Arthur always drove with his hands at ten-and-two. He checked his mirrors at regular intervals and physically turned to observe his blind spots whenever he changed lanes. The one thing he never did, obviously, was drink and drive. In fact, Arthur never touched a drop of alcohol in his entire life. He wasn't a prude about it. Arthur wasn't an evangelist of abstinence, he simply did not perceive any benefits to ingesting the liquid, and knew all too well, the devastating consequences.

As a young adult, mobile and employed, Arthur decided it time to complete his high school education and enrolled in a weekend program at the community college in the next town over. Monday to Friday he laboured at the mill; Saturday and Sunday he attended classes. He did not mind the lengthening of his already long weeks, in fact, Arthur rather enjoyed the new endeavour, for soon into his program he developed an affection for his instructor, Ms. Annabelle Hastings, a conservative woman of only four-years his senior. Her hair was golden as the fall harvest; her eyes as miraculous as the green flash of a perfect sunset. Nevertheless, being the son of his father, he did not act on his longings until he obtained his diploma.

When he finished his education, some full year later, he wasted no time in establishing a courtship with, then proposing to, and quickly marrying the woman who stood his world still. Their journey together was a fairy tale and keeping with his father's example he treated her his queen. Every Sunday Arthur would buy fresh flowers and, in the evening, after dinner, would take her on a romantic date—and continued to do so even after Annabelle birthed their first and only son, Henry. If you do the things you did at the start of the relationship, there will never be an end.

By all appearances, the Miller's were a model family, even down to the white picket fence. When Henry was old enough to go to school, Annabelle returned to her own classroom. Arthur accepted a promotion as the manager of the mill which guaranteed each weekend free to spend with his family. They wanted for nothing more.

Henry excelled in mathematics, while demonstrating superb athletic capabilities. He captained every scholastic team he played on and was looked up to by his peers. Like his father, he stayed away from intoxicants, and held a deep civic responsibility. Upon graduating high school, Henry enlisted with the 3rd Battalion Royal Canadian Regiment and moved to Garrison Petawawa. There he was readied for deployment to Afghanistan.

Both of his parents were extremely proud, and although Arthur did not display the 'My son is an Honour Student and Infantryman' bumpersticker he'd secretly purchased at the recruitment office, he did keep it bound to his visor beside his parent's fading picture.

During this time, Annabelle's doctor discovered a concerning lump in her breast and referred her to a specialist. Under compassionate authority, Henry's deployment was deferred until his mother's biopsy results were returned. Fortunately, the results were negative, the tumour was benign, and all was well. With all relieved, Henry deployed to Afghanistan for his first tour of duty.

Near the end of his experience, while on patrol outside Panjwa'i, Henry's section was ambushed and Henry caught a piece of shrapnel in the back of his head. He returned in a flag-draped coffin.

Needless to say, Arthur and Annabelle were devastated, spirit void, ghosts. Arthur, while fraught with reimagining's of his parent's murder and now his son's—for Annabelle—he remained the cornerstone for their mourning marriage.

Annabelle took leave from teaching as she was too distraught to be around children who would grow into noble young adults like her Henry had. She remained in the home mostly, too burdened to do much of anything else. Soon, that benign lump was benign no longer. The doctors learned that it had been cancerous from the start and was now metastasized in her lungs and heart and most of her chest.

In six months, she died.

Inside of a year, Arthur had lost his pride and joy, Henry and Annabelle, and was suddenly most alone.

After the funeral, he requested a two-week leave of absence from the mill in order to collect himself. He assured the owners that he would return fully prepared to fulfill his duties without distraction. Arthur had not requested a day off, nor had he been sick in all the years from when he first set foot inside the textile mill when he was sixteen.

The owners granted his request, and as Arthur assured, when he returned, he was renewed and composed to manage once again. The owners, however, in the time Arthur had been recovering, filled his position with a college graduate who was better qualified and came at a lesser salary. Arthur was given two-weeks severance and dismissed with a handshake.

He drove home in a daze, his mind completely consumed with the utter unfairness of being let go. His daze became anger then wheeled into bargaining, which led to depression, and by the time he'd accepted his dismissal, a horn blared his attention and Arthur swerved to right himself in his lane. He pulled over immediately, hands gripped tight on the steering wheel, and clenched his eyes. Arthur inhaled a deep breath and let it go, blowing all the air out. He turned off the ignition, unbuckled his seat belt and checked over his shoulder before opening the door. Arthur thumbed the lock-knob locked and started the familiar walk home.

He retired to his bedroom, sat on his side of the bed, and sighed. With no one left to be strong for, Arthur allowed himself to cry.

So overdrawn were his tears, his eyes swelled and stung with release. He cried with his face in his hands, tears burning down his wrists and to his elbows which soaked two circles on his trousers. His chest heaved with gasps as all the losses rushed forth. Arthur cried until he could cry no more. He rubbed his face and smoothed his cheeks. He bit his knuckle as he rested his chin on his clasped hands. Outside was getting dark. He sat there thinking. What he thought was to sit there until he knew what to do.

With the sun set, he concluded that in the morning he would pick up a newspaper and start looking for a new job.

He hummed his approval and pushed himself erect to carry out his ablutions before bed. Maybe it was how fast he stood, perhaps his legs were asleep having sat so long; whatever the reason, Arthur lost his balance. His skull connected with the corner of the dresser and then with the hardwood floor, where he died in a puddle of his own blood.

The Flame

It shouldn't be much longer. They say you know at the end, and maybe I believed that—I certainly do now—only I never gave it much thought before. Darkness surrounds me. If I summon the strength to flap my wings, just enough for my feet to leave the ground, they simply grate against the metallic walls and sound like a mouse clawing from inside an aluminum pail. One of those human-made devices: a small wooden bridge balanced on the lip of a bucket that gives way toward the cup of peanut butter centre of the inch-deep water around. The mouse drowns of exhaustion knowing if only that last step wasn't taken, freedom would still be had. And freedom is life.

In the beginning I struggled daily, beating my wings until I was sure they'd fall off. Whenever I made flight, I'd crash into the ebony ceiling or collide with the sleek containing walls. This led to lying shocked on the lip I now find myself, reduced to crawling in circles.

Below is a foul chamber, traced with the scent of fuel oil; if I don't die of starvation, surely, I will of this subtle poison. Already my breaths are short and reserved, for each time I inhale my head becomes lighted and any cognition I maintain evaporates. I wake up in this nigrescence, a place inky beyond the deepest cave or clouded moonless night. Alone; needless to say: I've become the mouse in the bucket, retracing my steps.

The new moon was third in its phase. The forest gleamed. In the distance, beneath the hallowed woods, a small flame flickered. Smoke ascended and the occasional crack of a wet knot heated sparked the sky. A little flame—one log, some smaller pieces—but a flame, still, on a cool moonlit night.

I made two passes over the warmth before settling in a shadowed tree, hung upside down in rest. Occasionally I'd dash off for an easy bite only to return to my inverted perch a moment later. A man with a wide-brimmed hat sat beside the fire. He didn't speak. He didn't drink. He didn't cook anything over the flame. Still, he appeared content, resting in the flickering light.

When the first drops of rain landed on the heated rocks and sizzled into mist the man simply raised his face to the sky, grinned, and continued to sit a while longer. Soon, the clouds opened wider and the droplets fell steadily. The man picked up a nearby stick and spread the ashes around. He lifted the main log onto the rocks and glanced at the sky one last time, smile still on his face, and turned to head into his modest cabin. I thought about this man, the shadow of gratitude he left in his place, and wondered if gratitude could really be that simple?

The rain poured. I issued waves in search of shelter. One returned from near the extinguished flame, a small hole, twice my size, dry and dark. I took flight and landed in the cold opening. I could not see inside, only that there was room to walk, and so I did, away from the exposed opening and free of the splashes of wet. How many times have I chastised myself over this? I could have bore the minor chill, but no, give me comfort upon comfort.

I screamed as the ground curved and became no more. I fluttered and flapped and flailed but I did not have the wingspan to give lift. The ground reappeared with a paralyzing thwack. For a minute I thought I'd landed outside, the orbs of light circled like stars. My vision cleared and I discovered myself here.

Returned to what brought me, my last steps. Any attempt to contemplate otherwise has proved futile. And so, I cried until the sobs became wails and the sound too great to endure, I was forced to abandon them also. An imitative thunder resounded in their wake, echoing inside this circular prison, forcing itself on me: what luck, cried the pitiful one.

I thought maybe if I closed my eyes—not that I could tell at first—but this was no aid as the only way I knew my eyes were closed is when they were, every wrong turn, not just this final blunder, but every misstep, every regret replayed in vivid colour. The only way to escape these torments are to keep my eyes wide open and await a darkness more complete.

Summer Love – An Acrostic

Always curious about what everybody else seemed to take for granted, Zach laid in bed and stared outside his window at the lone leaf still clinging to its tree. Birds had long abandoned their nests, leaving clumps of brush and hair and scavenged strips of plastic grocery bag silhouetted against the grey sky. Could today be the day he braved going to school? Did he dare risk seeing her? Everything teetered on this last question.

Four months and then: I don't love you anymore; as if love were something that could simply evaporate. Gosh! He rubbed his face with his hands and pressed his cheeks together.

"I still love you," he whispered, holding his face in fear of crying again. "Just like I have since…since, always."

Kali and he had met in the summer, at camp. Lake Louise: the fun, impactful summer adventure. More like: introduce you to your soulmate, share seven blissful days together before being whizzed off to ninth grade, where not even three months into the new school year she says, "I'm not sure anymore," camp.

No, it was: "I don't love you anymore."

On the third day of camp, during the nature hike, after two days of sneaking glances and shielding smiles, Kali and Zach had finally found themselves alone, side-by-side, and shy. Passing a patch of pink and red and purple wildflowers, Kali broke the silence and asked, "Would you pick me one?" Quick to act, Zach had knelt in the flowers in search of the right one for her.

Red, always red, he thought, carefully picking the only six petal starflower he could find.

She blushed, sniffed the sweet aroma, tucked it in her hair behind her ear and made Zach promise they would press it later so it would last forever. That night, they snuck off and pressed the flower into the pages of "A Treasury of Great Poems," even though neither of them cared too much for poetry, only figured couples as in love as they were deserved to have their memories stored among treasures. Unsure who should keep the book, they buried it near the lake's edge. Vows were exchanged, a map was drawn and then torn in half so each would need the other to retrieve it.

Worn now from keeping it in his pocket all this time, Zach held the map against the window and traced his finger along the dotted path.

"X marks the spot with a circle and a dot," he said. "Yeah right."

Zach pulled the covers over his head with a sigh and promised, tomorrow, maybe, he would try to get out of bed, again.

Reckoning – A Reverse Acrostic

Zooming across the bridge, Michael massaged the clutch and slipped his jubilee blue Honda CRX into fourth gear. Young people the world over, having grown up on Mario Kart and Need for Speed, intuitively know that the goal for any racer is to be in the gear that will support the fastest acceleration at any possible speed. Xers, like Michael's dad, hold to the tried and true, shifting between 2500 and 3000 RPM, regardless the objective. When driving in the city, sure, that will save the most fuel; but if you're in a qualifier and desperate to shave as many fractions of a second off your time, the red line is your best friend. Vinnie Miller, the professional stock car driver currently rocking Number 78 in the NASCAR Xfinity Series, swears by it. Unless you're racing at Vinnie's level, *or*, if you ever want to race at Vinnie's level, it's probably a good idea to follow his advice.

Take that to the bank.

Sorry dad.

Red dust erupted behind Michael's car as he roared onto the hard pack clay on the other side of the bridge. Quickly as he shifted for the straight away, the upcoming bend had him questioning, "Is this a third or fourth gear turn?" Patient, calm and cool, Michael dropped the shifter, smirked as the engine whined up to 6000 RPMs, and entered into a control drift around the bend. Only a mile to go, as the crow flies, fourth gear, fifth gear, sixth gear, and his spot on the amateur circuit would be secured. Never had he felt so confident in his own ability, in his car's ability, as he approached the finish line. Michael's father would have been proud. Levelling the steering wheel, hands holding firm but not tight, Michael peered through the windshield and strained to make out his mom and little sister among the cheering fans either side of the finish line.

"Kin is all you've got in this world," his father used to say; is what his father last whispered to him moments before he gasped his final breath from that sterile ambulance stretcher the previous August.

Just then, Michael struck a soft spot on the roadway—something which might not have been an issue if his eyes had been on the road—but now, unfocused, caused his CRX to waiver. In an instant the finish line swerved from view and was replaced by the confounding sight of the bridge he'd just crossed. Half a turn later and Michael was, again, panning the crowd. Gyrating toward the finish, Michael clung to the wheel, sucking back giant breathes, praying to anyone who could hear him, to please, keep his car from flipping end over end.

Finally, the tires caught and shuddered the momentum to a stop. Everyone in the crowd held their collective breaths as they stood stunned—half thankful the course hadn't stolen another living soul— half downcast at the opportunity missed in spinning out within reach of the finish line.

"Don't cry," Michael said, head resting on the wheel, body trembling.

"Count to ten, put on your proud face, this isn't giving up," his dad often consoled and now echoed in his ears. "Be the man your family needs you to be, on and off the course."

And with that, Michael reached outside the window, grabbed the door handle, opened the door, and stepped out proud, helmet tucked under his arm, and waved to the crowd—but mostly to his teary-eyed mom and little sister.

Atonement

It was February 29 again, and I was wondering which member of my family would try to kill me this time. Still, a small part hoped that maybe this year would be different from the past. I mean, it's been 16 years. I've made peace with what I did. It never had anything to do with them anyway. But here I was, lying awake in bed before my alarm and I couldn't help wondering if when I opened my eyes one of them would be standing above me, axe cocked behind their head, waiting to make sure the last thought that went through my mind would be they got me like they said they would.

I felt Michael stir. He'd be awake any minute. Surely, they wouldn't do it in front of him. They'd have to kill him too. The only guilt he had was that of association with me. He wasn't even in the picture when it happened. He has nothing to do with this. There's no way they would do it now.

Not a day goes by where I don't doubt my decision. That I wish it was me that died instead of him. That at least he died.

"Are you awake?" Michael whispered.

Did I say that out loud?

He rolled over and slid his body up to mine. I could feel his morning passion pressed against my thigh. He kissed my neck gently then nibbled my earlobe. His hands traced my hips.

"Good morning Beautiful," he said.

I pretended to be asleep. He knew I was awake.

He continued. He slipped a finger under my waistband, paused, and then allowed his hand to follow through. I pressed my head back lightly to expose my neck. He took the invitation.

His two fingers explored my wetness below as our tongues wrestled for dominance above.

That's when I jumped up.

"What are you doing?" he asked.

"Did you hear that?"

"Hear what?"

"I think someone's in the house."

Michael sighed and fell back onto the bed.

He didn't say anything.

Maybe he was right. Maybe there wasn't anybody in the house.

"What's going on, Jess? You've been acting strange all week."

"Nothing's going on. I just thought I heard something. I felt something."

"Yeah," he chuckled. "That was me inside of you."

"Don't be an idiot. I'm being serious."

"So am I. We were close to doing something we'd done every morning for the last six months, and then this week rolls around and I can barely get a kiss out of you."

"It's not like that."

"Then what's it like? Because this isn't the Jessica I fell in love with."

"Stop being so dramatic."

I listened for what I thought I heard: the brush of a sleeve across a bare wall; that one creak the floor only makes when someone steps on that exact spot; the breath of a shadow in the corner of the room. Anything.

"You're distancing yourself from me. There's a disconnect. It's not just the sex." He sat up. "Jessica, I've been in situations before that I've ignored and it only got worse. I don't want to do that again. We need to talk about it."

"What are you saying?"

"The closer we get to our wedding day, the more it feels like you're running away."

"Are you kidding?"

"It's serious."

If he only knew.

"I don't remember when it started, but you don't look at me like you used to."

He sounded like such a girl.

"There used to be love in your eyes," he said. "It was enough to just be around you. I never doubted you for a second. Now that we're a month away it's like you're second guessing us; like you're checking out. Now when I look in your eyes all I see is resentment, like I'm stealing your life from you."

"There you go again, making it all about you."

"Jessica, I'm not trying to make it about me. I'm sharing how I feel. I'm scared. I miss you. I miss us, Jess. I love you."

I hated when he said "I love you" at the end of his thought. It always made me feel I was obligated to say it back.

I placed my feet on the floor. The shock of the cold wood invigorated my legs.

"Please don't just walk away."

"I have to get ready for work."

#

The comforting smell of freshly brewed coffee filled the bathroom mixing with the steam of the hot shower. For a moment I forget to remember the inevitability the day will bring. I turned off the water. What could I do? Tell him? I couldn't tell him. He'd never believe me. Nobody does. I don't even believe me.

#

My mug sat beside the coffee pot. There was a bowl of sliced kiwi and strawberries on the table. Michael stood at the stove frying eggs.

"Thanks," I said.

"Of course. Eat up."

I thought about stepping behind him and nestling my head into his back, or kissing his neck like he had done to mine this morning; then I saw the note on the fridge:

Thirty days hath September,

April, June and November;

All the rest have thirty-one,

Excepting February alone

Which hath but twenty-eight, in fine,

Till leap year gives it twenty-nine.

"Did you write this?"

"What?"

"The poem. Did you write this here?"

"What do you mean, 'did I?' Who else would have?"

"Why'd you do it?"

"Because it's February 29ᵗʰ. We only get like 20 in a lifetime. It's a magical day."

"Well, the people in Scotland believe that if you're born on a Leap Day, your life will be an everlasting stream of suffering and pain."

#

How is anyone supposed to know what to do? Seriously. How do you know if the decision you make is the right one? Isn't it enough to at least have had the courage to make a decision? It has to better than not making a decision, right? Don't they see that? Can't he see that I'm distancing myself from him for his own sake? To protect him. If only he knew. Christ. If only he *knew,* then there'd be no way he would love me. There's no way he could. I should have never let it get this far to begin with. I don't even love myself. How am I supposed to love anyone else? I just need to make it through the day. Just one day.

Just today.

#

I didn't feel my head strike the steering wheel, but it struck. I opened my eyes to a half dozen blank faces staring at me. My foot was pressed on the brake and somehow, I was in the middle of a lifeless intersection.

The cracked giant grill of a white SUV glared at me in the rearview mirror.

I pounded the steering wheel with my fist. Why today?

I stepped out of the car and approached the vehicle behind me.

It was a woman. An Asian woman. She stared straight ahead. There was a young girl seated beside her.

"You have to be kidding me," I said. "Why did you have to be the goddamn stereotype?!"

Neither of them spoke. A black Mustang pulled up beside me. It was a young couple.

"We saw everything," the girl said. "She was on her phone. She sped past us and straight into you. Do you want our number in case you need a witness in court?"

"Thanks."

"Are you OK?" the girl asked. "You don't look too hot. Maybe you should sit down."

#

"I came as soon as I heard, baby. Are you OK?"

The fluorescent lights forced me to squint. I could barely make out the face, but I knew the voice: Michael. I looked around the room.

"You shouldn't move your neck like that. They're worried you might have a fracture."

"Fracture? From what?"

"From your face hitting the steering wheel. Don't you remember?"

"I think so."

"You were rear-ended. Apparently, you were coherent for the first couple of minutes after the accident, but then you collapsed in the street."

"Jesus. Is my car OK?"

"Your car? You could have a broken neck and you're worried about your car?"

"Don't lecture me, it was just a question."

"Sorry. I guess I'm still a little upset about this morning. When I got the call, I thought the worst, I was terrified." He paused. "Your car is a write off. Insurance will get you a new one."

"Oh. That's good."

"Were you on your phone when it happened?"

"I'm not doing this right now. You can stay, but I'm not doing this right now."

#

In a fog. Michael's voice was accompanied by others.

"How long has she been out for?"

"She was awake for a couple of minutes when I first arrived, but she's been asleep ever since." That was Michael. "Maybe a couple of hours?"

"How was she when she woke up?"

"Honestly," he said. "She was in a mood."

"That's Jessica for you. Once she digs in her heels there's no talking with her."

The voice sounded like my dad's voice.

My dad!

I had to wake up. Why couldn't I wake up?

"Are Julie and Paige coming?" Michael said.

"Yes, we all came together. They're talking with the doctor right now. Julie's worked with him before and you know how Paige is, always trying to network, so she's stuck to Julie's hip."

They laughed.

"Paige has got to be close to finishing nursing school, isn't she?"

"Final year."

"That's great, Stan. You must be proud."

I imagined my dad grinning ear to ear. He had the smile of a politician.

"And how about you two?" he asked Michael. "Are you all set for the big day?"

"Just a matter of time now. I'm actually looking forward to it being over with. Get on with our lives. I think the pressure is weighing on her."

"Hang in there, son. Julie was the same way during the month leading up to our wedding day. That was twenty-five years ago now."

"That's incredible. You don't see too much of that anymore."

"You sure don't. But here we are, living proof."

I pictured his big grin again. It's not that hard to stick together when you and your spouse are both psychopaths. I needed to open my eyes. Why'd Michael have to call them? Why today?

"Do you need to take a leak or anything? Have you left her side since you got here?"

"Thanks. If you don't mind, I've been holding it since I got here," Michael said.

"Take your time, stretch your legs. We'll be here when she wakes up again."

#

I felt a presence hovering over me. It descended closer. I felt its breath warm my face.

My body quivered.

"Hi Sweetie," my dad said. "Daddy's here now. Everything is going to be OK. Can you believe it's February 29 again? How does the old poem go? Excepting February alone, which hath but twenty-eight, in fine, till a leap year gives it twenty-nine."

He kissed my forehead.

"Rest now, little girl. You're going to need all the strength you can muster."

#

"Did you get it?" my dad asked.

"Of course," my mom said. "Where's Michael?"

"Giving his legs a stretch."

"Is she awake?"

"It's hard to tell," he said. "I whispered in her ear and I thought I noticed a quiver, but I don't know for sure." Then he snickered, "She'll wake up in hell soon enough."

"I want to be the one that gives it to her." That was Paige. "I am the nurse after all."

"All right Sweets, it's all you," my dad said.

Paige moved around the bed. She stopped when she reached my side. She cupped my hand. The gentleness of her touch surprised me. She leaned into my face.

"You won't notice right away," she said, "but you will soon enough. You'll be awake. You'll feel everything. But you won't be able to move. You'll be screaming out of your eyes for us to stop and nobody will be able to hear you. You're going to wish you were dead – but look around Jessica, you're in the hospital. Their only job is to keep you alive."

I heard my parents chuckle. I felt a coolness being carried through my veins. It reached down to my toes. It reached to the top of my head. Paige must have injected something into the IV.

"How do we know if it worked?" my dad asked.

"Well," Paige said, "If she opens her eyes and doesn't scream it worked."

I didn't open my eyes. I felt Paige holding my hand. I tried pulling it away. I couldn't. She took my pinky finger, straightened it out, and rested something on the tip below the fingernail. I felt pressure. Why couldn't I pull my hand free? A spike ran up my finger, up my hand, up my arm and into my shoulder, like when you press a tack by accident, my arm wanted to recoil but couldn't. I wanted to scream but nothing came out. My eyes welled and then shocked open. My family started laughing. The pain tripled. Paige continued to press the needle under my nail. I was losing my breath. Inside I was shaking but I knew it didn't show.

"What if she passes out?" my mom asked.

She sounded sincerely concerned.

"Just give her a little ephedrine."

"You girls are sick," said my dad.

"You're just jealous I came up with the idea," Paige said.

"Just wait till it's my turn."

#

My finger throbbed. Paige pressed my hand against the bed and snapped the needle. Its crisp crack bounced around the room. It felt like my finger had been sliced in two.

Paige replaced the medical sensor to cover the wound. My fucking sister. My parents. How could they do this to me? What else were they going to do?

A pricking burning scorched my veins. Fire blazed from my fingertip. I thought maybe like in a hot spring if I just didn't think about it and didn't move, the pain would go away. I couldn't move, but not think about it? How could I not think about it? I may as well have been strapped to a bed in the Toy-Box Killer's torture dungeon the way my psychopathic family was eager to pounce.

Where's Michael? Why did he leave me with these monsters? MICHAEL!

#

"Paige," my mom said. "Stand by the door and wait for Michael."

"No fair," she said. "I was just getting started."

"We have to move quick; and we have to take turns. This is the first time we get to do it together. Go wait at the door."

I watched Paige smirk as she walked across the room.

"Your turn Julie," my dad said. "What are you going to do?"

"Watch and see."

I knew the voice. She was a little girl about to poke a cat with a stick she spent hours sharpening in anticipation.

Her bulbous nose nearly touched mine. She kept it angled in arrogance as she calculated what she would say next. The light of the room ignited the tiny hairs above her lip and I knew if I could laugh at her for this it would send her into a rage.

"Hi Jessie," she said. "I wish I could say 'mamma loves you,' but, well, we all know that isn't true."

I wanted to spit in her face.

"Oh, look Stan," she said. "You can almost see the fear in those little blue eyes of hers."

My dad moved in for a closer look. He hummed. "Isn't that cute."

"OK," my mom said and pushed him aside. "It's my turn."

She flashed a razor in front of my face. It was a razor from my dad's shave kit. The kind of razor that comes individually wrapped in wax paper, both sides of the blade sharpened to slice with ease.

"Your face isn't as bloody as I hoped it would be," my mom said. "But that's life, isn't it? I'm just going to have to make the best with what I've got, you know, play the cards I'm dealt."

She used one of her hands to palm my face.

She set down the razor and unbuckled the neck brace.

She stroked my neck.

She wasn't going to slit my throat, was she? She couldn't. That would be too easy. She wanted me to suffer. Isn't that what all these years have been about? To make me suffer for what I did? To make me suffer beyond the hell I put myself through every day? I did what I had to do. I shouldn't have to pay for it over and over and over again.

Don't.

Please mom, don't do this. I'm sorry. I really am. Mommy, please stop.

I felt the sting when the razor pierced my skin. My heart raced. I saw my mom's eyes shimmer. Her lips tightened to expose her sunken cheeks and hollow bags beneath her eyes. She stared at me.

"Relax Darling," she said.

The sting dragged along my throat, then stopped.

OK. That's OK. That wasn't so bad.

My mom snapped her fingers in front of my face. I hadn't noticed I'd averted my eyes.

"This is going to hurt," she said. "But I need you to hang in there, baby. Paige has more to do and Daddy still needs his turn."

I felt the razor dig into the slit. My mom pressed so hard against my neck I thought she would break it. A crack exploded the room. The pressure gave way. I gasped for air. I tried to reach for my throat, but my arms remained limp by my side.

"Pass me the tracheotomy tube, Hun," she said.

The room began to fade. I couldn't hear. I couldn't breathe. My skin felt blue. There was more pressure on my throat. It was like choking on a chip that was being forced deeper and deeper inside me. The tissue grated like shredding cheese. My lungs burned. I sucked liquid copper. The taste filled my chest. And then I caught my breath. My vision returned. My mom tightened the neck brace and began petting my hair.

"There, there, Sweetie, there, there. Mamma fixed you up real nice." She smiled. "I think I may have dropped the razor inside before I ran the tube down though. Oops. Let me know when it starts to feel like drowning. It should be a little harder with each breath. Each nick of the blade on the inside of your lung will add just a little more blood. How many litres can they hold? It's been a long time since clinical anatomy. What I do know for sure is: your chest will get heavy. You'll taste it in your throat. You'll want to cry out for help but no one will be able to save you. No one will be able to save you like that dying child you abandoned. What do you think his last minutes were like? Do you think he cried out for a mommy that wasn't there? Do you think his begging landed on deaf ears? You'll know his pain Jessica. Mark my words. You will know his pain."

#

"Do you remember when Jessica was just a little girl and we were going to that Mexican restaurant all the time?" my dad said.

"Of course, Mya Riviera," said my mom.

"It must have been her second birthday. She kept shovelling those tortilla chips into her mouth when all of a sudden she burst out screaming bloody murder."

"Bone chilling."

"All the wait staff ran over. All the tables stared. We thought she dipped it in the habanero sauce so we made her drink milk but she kept on screaming; those gumball tears pouring down her face."

"I ran her to the bathroom and found that chip lodged in the back of her throat, its sharp corners digging in like anchors. She spat up blood."

"It was terrifying," my dad said.

My throat was on fire. My chest pooled. The room was closing in.

"Did I take it too far with the razor blade?" my mom asked.

"No, Julie. It was perfect." He pulled her in for a kiss. "I love you baby."

"I love you, too, Stan."

"Get a room," Paige said.

Everybody laughed. Everybody was always laughing.

"Glad to see your spirits are high," Michael said.

So stupid. How could he leave me alone with these monsters?

I choked. Blood splashed the inside of the tracheotomy tube. Michael ran to my bedside.

"What's going on? She's bleeding out of her tube," he paused. "Wait, why is there a tube in her throat?"

"She started choking while you were out. They cut a quick trach to keep her breathing. They think maybe a rib impaled one of her lungs when she hit the steering wheel."

"Jesus."

"I know. I hate seeing her like this," my mom said. "I'm torn though."

"What do you mean?"

"She wasn't wearing her seat belt."

"How do you know?"

"There's no abrasion or bruising across her chest," my mom said. "There would be if she was wearing her belt."

"Christ."

"I don't know how many times we told her to buckle-up when she was a kid. She just never listened. Life is a cruel teacher."

"I don't know Julie. That seems a little harsh. I mean, look at her."

Michael looked like he was going to cry. He loved me. I knew he did. I just didn't know why.

"She has her ways," he said, "and don't get me wrong, I'm not always a fan of those ways, but she's a good person. I'd never wish this on her in a million years."

Paige hugged him. She rubbed his arm and shot me half-cocked smile.

"Oh Michael," Paige said. "Mom didn't mean it like that. We all adore Jess. It's why we're here. And you, mister. You are just the sweetest, most stand-up guy. She's lucky to have you."

"Don't be silly," Michael said.

"For serious. I mean, if I'm being honest, it's crossed my mind a few times that if things didn't work out between the two of you, I just might have to take a turn."

Michael squeezed her close. He kissed the top of her head. "OK little sis."

Everybody laughed, again.

#

I was 18 when I met him. Not Michael, Shelly, and it was love at first sight. My world stopped spinning. It was as if all the pieces had finally fallen into place. I know it sounds cliché, but it was real. I was smitten. He treated me like the only girl in the world. When he looked in my eyes, I <u>knew</u> I was the only girl in the world. I wanted to be his forever.

We moved in together right away. Like, within weeks. The first day in the apartment, we were setting up the bedroom and he picked me up against the mattress and made love to me until we fell to the floor. It was amazing. There was always that passion between us. We were consumed with each other. We made meals together. We walked together. We talked even. How many people have a passionate relationship where communication is a cornerstone?

Right from the start we wanted to have children. And right from the start we were pregnant. I still remember the look on his face when I woke him up to tell him the news. Tears filled his eyes. His cheeks puffed an honest smile. He pulled me close and kissed my forehead. He said, 'I love you, Jessie. I love you so much.'

And I felt sick.

Here I'd found the greatest man in the world and I couldn't even be sure the baby was his.

#

"Kiss your fiancé then take me to the cafeteria. Your little sister is famished."

"Is that so?" Michael said.

"It is," Paige said.

I swear I saw her bite her bottom lip.

Michael leaned above me. "You heard your sister, Jess," he said.

"We're going to get the family some food, and you some flowers. You're in good hands here."

He kissed my forehead.

Please don't go Michael. Please. I need you.

"I love you," he said.

And I knew it would be the last time I heard anyone ever say that to me again.

#

Even with my eyes wide-open, my vision faded in and out. I got lost in a day-terror picturing my sister holding Michael's arm as they walked down the hall. She was telling some silly story or laughing at everything Michael said even though he wasn't being funny. They'd pass an empty room in an adjacent hallway and she'd bump him through the open door. Michael would laugh and turn to leave but she'd be advancing. He'd object at first, but he's a guy, and despite my sister being a bitch, she has always been pretty. She'd press him against the bed and run her hands down the front of his pants. She'd tell him how she knows things weren't going great in our relationship and how he deserves better and how he doesn't have to reciprocate she only wants to service him; help him relax a little. His pants would drop to the floor and she'd kneel in front of him knowing there was nothing left of his resolve.

A solid mass struck the side of my face. I was jarred from my daydream as a numb, eye watering nausea settled into the back of my skull.

"Stay with us Jessica," my dad said.

"Maybe we should give her a few milligrams of ephedrine," my mom said.

"Yeah. There's a good chance she'll pass out on my go."

The room became brighter. The metronomic sound of my heart on the monitor quickened. I could hear surgical tools being placed in metal pans somewhere outside the room. My eyes darted in every direction consuming my surroundings. The IV bag hung full. The TV remained off. The curtains were pulled back. The room was only my mom, my dad and me.

"Let's see what you brought," she said.

"You think you can handle it?"

"Bring it on."

He shuffled around and said, "I call it 'The Show Stopper.'"

My mom cocked her head in disbelief as if she wasn't quite sure what she was looking at.

The finger monitor squeezed my pinky. The razor floated with each breath I took to cut just a little bit more of my insides. But I was right. As long as I didn't move, which I couldn't, the pain was present but not intolerable. All I needed was for Michael to walk in while my dad was doing whatever he was about to do and this would all be over. I only had to last a few more minutes. I could last a few more minutes. What's a few more minutes?

"What have you done to my vibrator?" my mom asked.

"Relax Julie, I figured after this we'll splurge on some new toys."

"You're sick."

"She doesn't deserve this?"

"Oh, she does, but," my mom paused. "Are you really going to fuck our daughter?"

"Paige is our only daughter," my dad said. "Jessica is a whore and deserves a whore's punishment."

"So, you're going to punish her by excessive pleasure?"

"See for yourself; tell me if you'd find pleasure in this toy."

I caught a glimpse of the purple device as he handed it to my mom. It looked like a regular vibrator: a blunt end for insertion, a handle to hold in position, and one of those tickler nubs for clit stimulation. It looked like the one Michael had bought me before he went away on that business trip.

"Turn it on."

My mom pressed the button and the vibrator sprung to life.

The motor hummed like a tattoo gun. The silicon shook in my mother's hand. Lengths of shining metal pierced the skin at a hundred miles an hour. The alternating blades looked like teeth ready to devour whatever they were put in.

An angular bit spun from the tip of the purple silicon. This was not a toy. This was a miner's tool. This device was designed to borough deep into parts unexposed to the light. It would slice clean through me.

"Holy Christ," my mom said.

"Didn't know I was so technically inclined, did you?"

"This will kill her."

"Isn't that what we want?"

"You're sick," she said. "And I love every sick bit of you."

She turned off the device and handed it back to my dad.

"The best part is," he said, "if it doesn't kill her, she'll never be able to shame this family again."

"Give me a kiss and I'll go see if Michael is ready."

#

I couldn't bare Shelly finding out the baby wasn't his. It would have killed him. I knew he'd love me and the child regardless, but every morning I'd see what I'd done; every day I'd see it in the baby's face. We would have been doomed to live unhappily ever after, because of me. Because of me and my insecurities. So, I pushed him away. I broke up with him. I told him I never wanted to see him again. I told him he didn't owe me anything. I told him: go.

He went to my parents. He begged for advice. Nobody could make heads or tails of the situation. They apologized to him on my behalf. They called me. They showed up at my apartment begging for answers and I turned them all away.

I don't know how they found out I wasn't keeping the baby, but they found out. I didn't abort or anything, I'm not a beast. I carried full term. I just gave him up at birth. I didn't know he'd be born sick. How could I? Those things happen. I didn't plan it. I made the decision to give him up before he was born. It wasn't my fault. I gave him up because I thought he deserved better. I was sorry I failed him from the start and only wanted to give him opportunity. I didn't think he'd get that with me. I did what I thought was best. I did. I…

Wait. Did she just say she was going to see if Michael was ready?

#

Inside I was thrashing to be free. I kicked. I pushed. I swung and scratched and clawed. Only my body wouldn't respond.

My dad pulled the sheet. He lifted my gown and stared.

"Looks a lot different from when you were just a little girl," he said.

My eyes filled with tears.

"Why do you look so sad, honey? Isn't this a position you're used to being in? Laying on your back, cunt exposed, eager? This is how they all did it, right?"

He hovered over my body and brought his face to mine. He bit his bottom lip. His hand traced the inside of my thigh.

I felt the warmth of a tear escape my eye and run down my cheek.

Please don't do this daddy.

He brought his mouth to my ear.

Please daddy, don't do this.

"I bet you're dripping with excitement right now," he said.

That first tear must have broken the levy. Both sides of my face were singed with a stream of water from my eyes.

I felt the sharpness in the base of my throat. My stomach convulsed but I couldn't vomit. The razor that was forced down by my mom was now being pushed in the opposite direction. The weight in my chest was squeezing the breath from my lungs and forcing the blade back up my throat. It was stuck. The corners anchored into the cartilage. The blade bent with the pressure and dragged along the rigid tissue. The air from the oxygen machine was the opposing force.

I was going to die. Please let me die. Please. I've suffered enough. Please. I'm begging.

#

"You can't put it in dry," Paige said. "You have to spit on it first." She paused and turned to Michael. "You're familiar with that aren't you?"

"You sound a little jealous Paige."

"You've been sleeping with my sister. You don't think I enjoyed that did you?"

"And you think I did? I was only doing it for you."

"Well aren't you chivalrous?"

"Get over here," he said.

Paige obliged.

Michael gripped her nape and stared her in the eyes. He grinned my dad's grin.

"I fucking love you Paige."

He pulled her face to his own and they kissed like Shelly and I used to.

"Let's put an end to this and get on with our lives," Michael said.

"I'll spit," said Paige.

She blew me a kiss and smiled.

Just Another Tuesday Morning

I was sitting at my desk, half-drunk on wine, freezing in my concrete jail of an apartment, and wondering what to do next.

She lay on the carpet, back facing me, huddled against the brown microfiber at the base of the couch. Black hair, black hoodie, black leggings, great ass. I kicked off the side of the desk and spun in my leather swivel chair. Probably the only piece of quality furniture in the dump. It's spinning I spotted the line on the bookcase that one of us had forgot.

Raised *waste not, want not*, I hurried to the corner of the room and nostrilled it back before she woke up. That's what you get for being a bitch—not a woman, I would never call a woman a bitch; no, someone who promises so much potential at the beginning of the three-day binge, but barely into the second day after drinking the last of the whisky before the liquor store re-opened in the morning and instead passes out on the wine stained carpet and nary the courtesy to spread her legs and let me dip inside a minute, but instead sidles up the couch and snores away, kind of bitch. Like a pussy.

Well, you lock into a bender with ol' Johnny Bradford, then you're going all the way, ma'am.

At least that's what I've been told. All-in-Johnny, or something like that.

I swallowed the drip, grabbed the bag of wine from the trash, and squeezed out a shot glass worth of Cabernet. I paced the room and chortled realizing I was pacing the room. The people below my apartment must have hated me.

For some reason, that thought, that little bit of wine, and that last line instilled a masculine confidence I've only ever experienced four times before in my thirty-three years on this shithole of planet.

Because I am a man, I can do whatever the fuck I want.

It's that moment when some over-confident nobody decides that today is the day where he won't take it anymore and finally stands up for himself against the meathead hitting on his girlfriend and cocks back to punch the cigar-face straight in his snout—and when he has and stands rubbing his fairy-fist in his other hand, he realizes he's just unleashed a whole lot of ugly into the world.

I'm the meathead.

And that's the male confidence America was built on.

U-rah!

Meathead doesn't have to kick the shit out of the pansy, though he could, and he wouldn't be wrong to do so—he can simply grin, narrow his eyes ever so slightly, palm his own mouth and stroke his chin once before shaking his head, sucking his lips and saying, "Now why'd you go and do something stupid like that?"

Meathead knows he doesn't have anything to prove, it's in his eyes. Instead, he returns his attention to the woman, come 'on baby, and takes her away. That's male confidence. To take whatever the fuck you want, because who's going to stop you?

And I felt it right then and there. Her laying lifeless on the floor. You're going all the way, bitch.

I one handed my belt and let the clasp hang. It jingled as I fingered the button on my jeans. I always wear Levi's, you know why? Because men wear Levi's.

Unzipped my fly. Grunted. Did it again. Primal.

#

We started this particular bender the way all benders begin. At the start: She showed up leaning against the door frame, hair tied back, eyeliner tight around her ice blue eyes, grinning daring-like and singsonging, "I've got a surprise."

She giggled raising a matte black gift bag over her head and pushed past me into the apartment. One of two ways this was going to go down, and both meant a broke bank account and bloody Kleenexes before we finished.

"You are literally fucking killing me how dick-ma-tized I am," she said cupping her full chest with a lift and wiggling slightly to readjust. Naked she has a little tag beside her left nipple makes it look like she's got three. It's her insatiable cock hunger that had me glued from the start. That she always showed up with blow and Jäger sealed the deal.

"When do you work next?" I asked in faux concern.

She already had a baggie untied and was using her laminated Blockbuster card to divvy up some lines.

"That's so cute," she whined. "You're trying to be responsible." She slapped the card on the table and handed me the candy cane striped straw. "Just sniff this and shut up. Girls' got needs."

In the bedroom she pushed me on the mattress, gripped my belt and yanked it free from around my waist. She bit over my boxers and moaned a depraved growl. Before I could say throat-fucker she had my purple onion pressed against her tonsils and tongue fluttering about lapping at my balls.

The only fucking thing I didn't overly care for about this broad and her eagerness is her imitating one-too-many a low-budget porno where the girls always slurp and gag and tear while hoovering. I mean, a professional could execute the same scene without a peep less the occasional blessed sigh and pleasing desired eyes. *Beggars can't be choosers*, and ol' Johnny Bradford ain't no beggar chump.

She's got me all edge of the precipice, soaked like a peddo at a preschool, down my shaft, coating my cue balls and lubing my ass when lighting jolt sears my eyes, my stomach contracts and my euphoria vanishes as fire explodes my anus.

I must have passed out it hurt so much 'cause when I opened my eyes, shit was not how I'd left it.

It took me a second, that smoothed purple baton resting on my lips, I squirmed and focused my eyes—discombobulated is a word right?— the Bitch was straddling my stomach, black strapped harness around her white pale skin with a 8-inch purple baton erect from where her vagina should have been, grinning.

"Guess you should have asked what the surprise was," she said with a shrug.

I pushed her off of me and sat up.

"It's called pegging, asshole," she pouted.

My ass stung. More than stung. My ass bled. Or at least it felt like it should be bleeding.

She stroked her purple shaft. "Don't be such a baby, *god*, I've pissed in your mouth before."

I dodged the remark. "Something goes in yours first."

"Anything, anytime," she said proudly, then sighed. "You're such a fucking buzzkill, you know that."

She looked kinda sexy, nude less the harness and throbbing silicon cock, and I told her so.

"'Moments passed, dick. I need a drink."

#

For a minute, I stood above her—not second guessing myself, more admiring the prize. It was religious. Felt along for her waistband, tucked both sets of digits inside. Her skin was supple, limp almost, but warm. The blood stirred in me.

The trick with getting a broad's pants off unnoticed while she's passed out is to take your time. You don't rush right in and yank the things down—she might wake up—then you're fucked.

Go slow, and if you wonder if you're going too slow, you're not. Slow down, do it again. The reward is always worth the effort.

Let me tell you, when I finally got her Lululemon spandex snug around her thighs, I was throbbing. If I caught a breeze I would have nutted.

A little bit of spit for the tip—you want to be a gentleman about it—then I rested the helmet on her cheeks. The thing was Crayola-purple against her My-fair-lady-white. She had a Jew star drawn in black Sharpie just below her hip. I released my grip and inspected my palm. Sure enough, a swastika.

I forget why we drew these ridiculous emblems on each other, but here they were, evidence of our ludicrous in the preceding hours. Something about using my righteous hand to slap her Jew ass—and the irony being, of course, my Shylock nose.

The blood lessened and the purple began to fade. I could fuck her any time I wanted. It would have been like stealing from a buffet. Goddamn permanent marker. Perfectly good ass. I patted her bottom as I thought what to do instead.

Okay, okay—you're going to think me crude, and maybe I was, but let me tell you: Jackson Pollock's art is crude and it sells for a hundred and forty million dollars.

I'm not saying I'm up there with Pretty Boy Pollock. I'm just saying, *she said*: anything, anytime.

Initially I thought about sticking the cap-end in first, probably some Pavlovian instinct because that's the end you write with—thank Christ for my lizard brain because suddenly I wondered what would happen when the damn thing uncapped inside? And you know it would because all those stories of fairy-fisted nobodies showing up in emergency having to undergo surgery because the Hot Wheel they inserted, the Pert shampoo bottle, the goddamn light bulb—hand to Christ—was there one moment, and for no fucking reason except the suppository wanting nothing to do with the pervert experience saw an opportunity and like a gofer in farmer Bill's potash field dove head first into the poop chute. You're damn straight the cap would have broken free and disappeared.

She would have had a fit, too, all stopped up, going to the doctors and finding a Sharpie permanent marker cap shadowed on her x-ray. Of course she would have blamed me.

Call it a science experiment. I spit in my hand. It took a couple times on account of all the blow we'd consumed. Ran the marker back-and-forth to lube it up, then poked the chocolate covered starfish.

A limp body, impossible to lift, is surprisingly welcoming to foreign objects. Soon as I set the spit-dripping grey tip of the Sharpie against the pinprick centre of the starfish, it relented. Spiralled open like a camera shutter and latched on like it was chewing a finger.

The entire thing caught me off guard. I paused. Hypothesized it needed a little more lube, then applied a gentle pressure. That's paramount. You have to be gentle. Just like not yanking the pants down, you have to go slow. More women would be open to ass-fucking if more men would just slow down. Slow down, do it again. Breathe. All that yuppie shit. Nice, slow, consistent pressure. Add a little more spittle, and before I knew it, I was breaking the cap line and almost out of marker when I thought maybe I should pull back a little, but as soon as the thought entered my mind, the son-of-a-bitch dove headfirst into the land of gofers.

For what must have been five minutes I just stared at her asshole. One minute it's a pinprick, a bunch of nondescript seashell crevasses spiralling towards her supple My-fair-lady-white ass cheeks, next minute it's dislocated its jaw to swallow a six-inch goddamn Sharpie, then bam! Pinprick again like it didn't just swallow a permanent marker.

I'm imagining her getting cramps after not shitting for two days: her bloated gut; a little seepage; how she'll go to the doctor, he'll snap the rubber glove, pop a finger in to pressure activate the rectum; trouble shoot with an x-ray and discover what couldn't be—is that what I think it is—there's no way—a Sharpie?—Hoover damming her intestines; starting to panic when the son-of-a-bitch shot out her ass cheeks like a heat seeking missile.

My laugh woke her up, "What are you doing?" I'm caught literally with my pants down, her ass exposed, so I tell her the truth, "I was going to stick it in your ass, baby."

She was in that perfect dream-wake state, not really sleeping but not really here, one-hundred percent suggestible, so I thought, *maybe*.

"Is there a star on my ass?" she asked. She thumbed at her waistband and tugged at her Lulu's. She tilted her hips and leaned closer into the couch. "I just had the weirdest dream about a Sharpie."

I sniggered.

She rolled over. Her eyes were evil, narrow, above her sinister grin. "I guess that means it's my turn now."

The Snowflakes Look Like People at Last

It was to be the greatest story ever written. It's how any noble venture begins. He wrote:

The rain struck the windshield as violently as a storm assaults a man's day, yet he persevered; a restrained smile accented the corners of his mouth as he listened to the normalizing cadence of the thump in the trunk.

Her breath brushed the hairs on his neck and removed his fingers from the keys.

"White male privilege," she said.

"What?"

"You're writing from a man's perspective. The narrative is unoriginal."

There was a time when interruptions would have sent him into a rage. This was not the time. Not with simple domestics destroying otherwise profitable lives.

"Explain," he said.

"A *man's* day. *He. His.* You're isolating women. You're isolating trans. You're perpetuating the white supremacist capitalistic patriarchy which permeates our very existence."

"It's a story."

"It's misogynistic."

He hung his head. Strike the desk? Strike his head? Strike her? No. He could only agree.

"What do you suggest?" he asked.

"The rain struck the windshield as violently as a storm assaults a person's day; yet perseverance was necessary. A restrained smile accented the corners of mouth as the normalizing cadence of the thump in the trunk continued."

"Who's the driver then?"

"It's open," she said. The person could be anybody, so the person becomes everybody."

"So, you can't relate to a male character in a fictional narrative."

"It's not about me," she said. "It's about giving voice to the marginalized."

"It's not a story about the marginalized."

"Every time you repeat the white supremacist capitalistic patriarchy agenda, you're furthering the narrative."

"So 'the rain struck the windshield as violently as a storm assaults a person's day; yet perseverance was necessary. A restrained smile accented the corners of mouth as the normalizing cadence of the thump in the trunk continued,' is inclusive?"

"No. It's still full of flaws."

He wanted a drink, but the day was only half passed and she would call him her father if he poured one before dinner.

"Explain."

"Don't infantilize me," she said.

"Infantilize?"

"It's when a man behaves condescendingly to a woman or anyone else, he thinks less-than-of."

"I don't think less-than of you," he said. "I've never had to consider all these details when putting a sentence to page before."

"That's because the narrative promotes your white privilege," she said. "It's always your little boys club."

"Give me your feedback."

"Why do you always have to use trigger words? Struck? Violently? Assault? Do you really have to force women to relive the trauma of their abusive relationships?"

"One in 3 men is in an abusive relationship also," he said.

"But it's not 1 in 4. You're a misogynist."

"How should I write it then?"

"The rain fell on the windshield as rain will in a storm; yet the driver drove on. A restrained smile accented the corners of mouth as the normalizing cadence of the thump in the trunk continued."

"It's lifeless."

"It says the same thing as it did before, only now it's not marginalizing the underrepresented."

"You're white middle-class."

"That has nothing to do with it," she said. "I'm not in the skin I am because I chose it."

"That's my point."

"So, it's OK to be a misogynist and a white supremacist and a capitalist and a bigot because you were born into it?"

"If you think I'm all those things then why are you with me?"

"You just need to be educated."

"So, educate me. Is the sentence good now? Can I move on?"

"Are you kidding? Windshield? Storm? Driver? Who's in the trunk?"

"Are *you* kidding?"

"The wind is natural. Why do you want to shield it?"

"You're being facetious now."

"Don't call me a fascist," she said. "You're the fascist for not making the driver a person of colour or of indigenous status."

"What?"

"There are other voices besides your boys club of white supremacist capitalistic male patriarchs."

"When have I ever aligned with white supremacists?"

"Don't micro-aggress me. You're a straight white male. It's ingrained."

"Says you?"

"Says the entire system."

"I can't do this."

"So, you don't want my input?"

"No."

"So, you're an anti-feminist then? You want it to be the day where rule-of-thumb was law?"

His jaw dropped; he had to physically lift it from the floor.

"You know that's not true."

"I don't know," she said. "It sounds like you hate women and like you're a little rapey."

"Rapey?"

"Who's in the trunk?"

"What?"

"The rain fell on the windshield as rain will in a storm; yet the driver drove on. A restrained smile accented the corners of mouth as the normalizing cadence of the thump in the trunk continued."

"The lover," he said.

"That's why you're a misogynist. The driver is a man and his girlfriend is in the trunk. What about gay people, or bisexual people or transgender people or gender fluid people?"

"Gender fluid?"

"Yeah, what about them?"

"I'm not writing about them."

"But if they pick up your book and read it, they'll feel marginalized and then you'll be perpetuating the white supre–"

"I can't be expected to write to everybody."

"You should try."

"Why?"

"Because the underrepresented need a voice and because you're so privileged you should give up some of your stature."

"Stature? I work just as hard as the next person."

"But it's easier for you to get a job."

"Easier? Every application I send to a human resources department specifically solicits anyone who identifies as an African-American, a woman, indigenous or immigrant, sexual preference, low-income, Islamic or disabled. It's becoming impossible to be a straight white male in this modern day."

"I'm going to pretend you didn't just say that."

"This is insane," he said.

"The rain fell as rain falls, and the driver drove on. A normalizing thump beat from the trunk."

"Isn't 'beat' abusive?" he said.

"This is one big joke to you isn't it?" she said. "Domestic violence is not a laughing matter."

"I know," he said. "My divorce was the result of my wife's violence."

"There you go again," she said. "Making it all about you. *My* divorce. *My* wife–as if she's a piece of property. *My* wife's violence. Don't minimize a woman's experience of domestic abuse in a relationship."

He held his head in his hands.

"The rain fell. The driver drove," she said.

"So, nothing happens. Is it safe to start from here?"

"What about people who have been in floods and are triggered by rain?" she said. "You can't write something knowing there are people who may suffer because of your words."

"So, the sun shines, then."

"No, because there are also people who have suffered from drought."

"The driver drove."

"But what if the person has never driven? Or is reading this in a plane? Or living on a boat? Or can't afford any of these luxuries and is walking? Or is disabled and can't even walk? What then?"

"You can't be serious," he said.

"You're patronizing me."

"What do I write then?"

"The person."

"The person, what?"

"Just the person," she said. "In fact, you shouldn't write at all. The market is over saturated with straight white males and we need to create room for a different narrative that doesn't come from the white supremacist male capitalist patriarchy."

"I hate that phrase."

"That's because it threatens your identity."

"I'm not a white supremacist or a part of the capitalist patriarchy."

"You think that because it's all you've ever known."

"Enlighten me to the other way."

"Men are violent and women are oppressed."

"You know I'm a man, right?"

"It wouldn't hurt you to be a little more effeminate."

"The person, then," he said.

"But what if the individual doesn't identify as a person?"

"What else would they identify as?" the man asked.

"It's not a choice to identify as something. It's a fact of life."

"So, the person could be a rock?"

"Stop saying 'the person.'"

"The."

"The, what?" she asked.

"From the entire introduction, 'the' is all that remains."

"Maybe. But 'the' implies something that isn't 'the.'"

"Then write my first sentence for me."

"Don't tell me what to do."

"I'm seriously just trying to learn."

"OK," she said. "If I was going to rewrite your sentence and remove all the bigotry and misogyny and violence and segregation, I would write:
—"

The blinking cursor laughed.

He closed the lid of the laptop and retreated to the kitchen.

The man poured himself a glass of orange juice and sat down at the table.

A restrained smile accented the corners of his mouth as he listened to the normalizing cadence of reason encourage him to raise a shotgun to his chin.

The Northern Republic

The morning the Northern Republic had finally strengthened beyond the divisiveness of gender, the world over applauded the enlightenment as humanity's greatest achievement. Feminists cheered their equality. The queers paraded. And by queers, I mean the L.G.B.T.Q.I.A.+, which includes all gay and lesbian, bisexual, pansexual, asexual, demisexual, graysexual, cisgender, transgender, trans* or trans+, gender nonconforming (g.n.c.), nonbinary, genderqueer, gender fluid, gender-neutral, the m.a.a.b./f.a.a.b./u.a.a.b. (male-assigned at birth/female-assigned at birth/unassigned at birth), intersex, and + (for those whom letters and words can't describe). Which includes the 2S+QTBIPOC bodies (two-spirit, black, trans, indigenous, and people of colour). But none of these titles existed yet, and they were all still just fags.

But this equality made everybody happy.

For a day.

Equality: The New Normal. The New Normal for the Northern Republic.

The grass beyond the fence was now the everywhere grass, as they had removed all the fences. And how plain did it all appear. Although nobody admitted it, there was a settling realization which clung to the earth like a great fog: the grass wasn't greener after all. Maybe it never was. The assumption was a lie. All the blasphemy about equality of outcome was empty as the words which represented them. The self-abhorred marginalized and underprivileged could not comprehend that equality required inequality to define itself. And what an oversight this was.

In pursuing a fictional utopia, the first step toward such a lofty goal was to eradicate masculinity. O how it became such a toxic word.

Masculinity, masculinity, masculinity—I can feel the shivers run down my spine even whispering the word now.

They began with the children, coercing the schools to remove all competition in their sports—which were all sports except for soccer; soccer has never been a sport, and for this reason permitted a viable outlet for children to take part in.

The children were herded into the sexless endeavour, guided by Christ's warning that the last shall be first and the first last: the least athletic were captains of their respective teams, the most athletic hobbled into positions of water-boy although it wasn't called water-boy, for that is masculine and masculine is toxic remember—the term became water-attendant. Do not fear, however, at the participant ribbon ceremony at the end of each season, water-attendants received the same ribbon as all the other soccer players, because all were equal.

The rules did not change, there were two teams though both encouraged the other team to win which was only achieved by an identical score, of say, for example, 0-0 or 1-1. Only once in the new history of the game did a match reach a final score of 2-2, and this only with the expert aid of three mindfulness sessions throughout the match. It is important to note that after this gut-wrenching highly stressful event; the sport was finally dropped from extracurricular activities as many of the students suffered tremendously, enormously, during the competition.

For historical accuracy, allow me to at least offer the details of the last of the faux sport. The grass was replaced with a softer, synthetic foam which resembled grass, green and reaching and all of that, but less assaulting than natural grass, the kind that stained clothing and caused the sniffles when cut, and what was probably the most repulsive feature of that grass, which played a significant role in eliminating it: grass could assault the ears when an unknowing child horrendously plucked a blade from the ground and tightened it between both thumbs, pressed lips to said tautness and expelled a blast of air. Ugh, the horrible shriek it made, they all complained. And that was the end of grass.

They replaced the soccer ball with a helium nitrogen balloon, lighter than air so it required less centrifugal force in propelling it down the field. It remained the same size as historical soccer balls, as did the field: technically, twice the size required for a fast-paced game. This ensured none of the players could come remotely close to each other and in doing so risk bodily contact. Nevertheless, should this unfortunate event occur, the players knew to fall to the ground in the most dramatic fashion. The brushed child would wail and roll and tighten their face to appear in the most tortured ailment imaginable and remain on the ground until the referee raised a coloured card-stock showing that a transgression had occurred. But this would only happen if the fallen player's teammates swarmed the referee, mimicking the display of the fallen player, begging the authority figure to intervene on behalf of their victimized comrade. These displays became quite the spectacle and were routinely recycled on the esteemed highlight reel.

During the first season—which was also the last season after that unfortunate 2-2 match—in fact, it was this 2-2 game; see, there was this youthful girl, a star, if there were stars, so soft-spoken, so petite and nonthreatening. Her wrists dawned all the colours of all the support bracelets ever pawned. What was most lovely about this youthful girl was her gender fluidity. Most mornings she was a girl, then in the afternoon he identified as a boy, and there is even some speculation that just before bed, he'd flow back to she and become a dragon before drifting off to sleep. My! The dreams the dragon child would have adventured in slumber. Most will agree, however, and though they would never speak it out loud in fear of provoking the slightest hint of animosity, but, it was secretly wondered if her dragon fluidity gave her an advantage in the sport.

Midway through this last game, the score a dreadful 2-1 for her team, the balloon drifted to centre field where she had been resting after having jogged several feet only moments before. She certainly didn't mean to. It wasn't in malice or anger. It was simply the unattached kick of a youthful girl indifferent to the outcome as all good youthful girls are. Poor thing. She swung her leg and kicked the balloon, and be it the wind, or the precise angle her foot connected with the near floating object, the balloon soared the length of the field and brushed the goaltenders cheek before floating into the back of the net. O how the crowd and the players shrieked in chorus. The scoreboard flashed 3-1. This girl collapsed and rolled in anguish. She screamed in terror. She held her ankle and foamed at the lips.

The poor child goaltender, who survived the brush with the balloon ball, likewise fell to the ground and clutched his face where the ball had struck. He wailed and moaned and put on such an exhibit he became tangled in the netting (which the kindly janitor—who was not called a janitor but a Cleanliness Barista of the Educational Enjoyment Centre—expertly cut him down from after the referee resolved the game).

Both teams swarmed the referee and guffawed and cried and waved their child arms, begging reparations for these victims. That poor referee. She did all that she could have done and with great solemnity she raised a red card-stock above her head, quieted the crowd and revoked the goal. But the crowd demanded more. As an exemplar of bravery, the referee awarded the goal to the injured goaltenders team. And everybody cheered. And that was the end of soccer. It had become just too dangerous.

The conclusion of the athletic holocaust marked the beginning of the Social Justice regime. But a regime is powerless without an emblem. Not oppressive power; rightful, just power. An image to separate those for and to demonize those against because what kind of monster would oppose social justice for all!

Much of the original fighting which gave rise to the Social Justice regime began of the feminist movement. Women who wanted to shed the shackles of homemaker and enter the workforce once and for all. Women who experienced life under the thumb of men and rejected heterosexuality for that of faggotry. They vilified everything man-made (for simplicity's sake, pretend there were at least *some* things which were not made by a man). And do you know who the greatest offender was?

Tampons.

That wad of absorbent material introduced into a body cavity or canal to absorb secretions, such as the red menstruation liquid, or to arrest hemorrhaging; or both. This revolutionary hygiene product introduced all the way back in the progressive year eighteen and forty-eight was symbolized as the Nero of toxic masculinity. Surely the new world order could not permit such a cancer.

Tear out your tampons! The bullhorns screamed. Free yourself from all toxic masculinity!

It seemed implausible anyone would adopt the mandate, but retrospect has a way of providing clarity where now it appears the only logical conclusion. Some sneered at the suggestion. Surely no one would commit such a disgusting act of self-immolation, but they were wrong.

The first lady, this brave woman, out in the world making her own way, commuting via public transport in the underground metro, proudly. Encased in that metal tube surrounded by men on their way to work and her being on her own way to work, the tube must have felt like a prison, or a ploy to contain her—whatever the pressure cooker ordered, it was enough to embolden her stand.

In flow, tampon eager to be plucked, she scanned the car, made eyes with each of the male passengers, then shoved her hand into the front of her pant suit pants. The onlookers turned away embarrassed, but only for a moment. She wound her delicate finger around the string and yanked with the force of a hundred years of oppression. The bloody wad sprang forth and dripped down her wrist from her high reaching hand. The men gagged. Many groaned. And if this were where the episode ended, that may have been the worst of responses. But no. This is not where it ended. This is where it began. This woman, Hilary Ramhod—yes! that was her name—she twisted her wrist like she was winding up a lasso. Round and round she spun the swollen mess it splattered the entire car red by the time the doors opened at the next stop. The gaggle rolled onto the platform covered in their own vomit and tepid menstrual red. Triumphantly, as the story goes, Hilary stepped forth, unmarred by any of the opposing fluids, only a red spot near the entrance to her birthing canal visible.

Thus became the symbol. It wasn't six hours before the nation had followed Hilary's lead and removed their own hygiene products. RSD's, they were dubbed: Red Spots of Defiance. Something like the Jew-band accessory worn proud under Hitler's reign. With us or against us!

It wasn't long before it positioned the fags to claim their own version of the symbol. Since the male anatomy does not provide the opportunity to shed birthing canal lining in a rivulet of red, the fags had to compromise. Since they ravenously sought throbbing penises to grind their excrement chutes upon, and since after several such poundings, the seal becomes sufficiently less a seal and thus as in traditional residential plumbing, leakage occurs, excrement chute seepage became the obvious correlative to the Red Spot of Defiance.

It began when two fags were dressing after a night of pounding, not having time to shower and still under the influence of MDMA (a drug which helps to forget the debaucheries and unnatural behaviour they have just taken part in or were about to) when the Power Bottom noticed trace seepage on his Tommy Hilfiger pleated shorts when twirling in the full-length mirror. Fags are the only known people who own full-length mirrors—if you were ever unsure if your comrade was a fag or not, this was a consistent indicator.

Rightly aghast at the discovery, he was even more infuriated to learn his playmate was out of bleach—it used to be a ritual to bleach their undergarments and pants daily and ultimately led to acid washing and artificial tears in the fabric. The unperturbed partner, the Top, flippantly said, "Wear it like a Red Spot of Defiance, boo," before browsing the Home and Garden Outdoor Kitchen issue he used for sexual stimulation when aroused without his Power Bottom nearby.

Obvious now, the Power Bottom cocked his head in Utilitarian recognition, pondered the idea, as if considering two shades of eggshell to repaint the nook. Defiantly, proudly, he decided exactly that this is what homosexuals everywhere needed.

Excuse me, I must apologize for my distasteful use of the derogative term *homosexual*. It's a word only fags can use when addressing each other in greeting, like "Sup, homo," and exclamation, "Homo please!" and when discussing another fag, "Do you know what that homo did?" Herein I shall purpose to use only technical terms.

We are discussing faggots.

It was a mark of their own. A mark to separate them from the oppressive patriarchy, which I obviously mean the white patriarchy as all sinister patriarchies are white in melanin. It was a mark to join with their oppressed sisters, who they envied so much, ironically not for their menstrual cycles, but with an innocent feminine admiration. Thus, the Excremental Chute Seepage spot was born, and for strictly administrative reasoning, both groups dropped their verbiage and adopted SPOTS as their self-proclaimed Jew-band.

An interesting aside, a year after the Spot movement began leaving its mark, a young faggot entrepreneur, son of two feminist dykes born possible only by an unnamed male sperm-donor, invented a pocket wipe which would remove and sanitize any material marred with either menstrual red or excrement chute seepage. He named it, smartly, "Make Room For My Spot," and sold millions to the entertainment venue.

I could belabour the complete history of how we arrived here, but lets just presume way leads onto way as it often does and the core seven groups finally claimed power. They were, technically named, the Feminists, the Fags, the Niggers, the Single-Mother Whores (or any welfare case), the Sand-Niggers (or anyone not born of the Republic), the Retards and Cripples, and the ISIS—who were lumped together because Islam was intuitively understood to cause all mental retardation and cripple female genitalia.

Each group sounded their own march over the community networks, and it was soon discovered that when played in succession of each other, together they formed the sparkling and complicated Villanelle; as if it were a sign of meant to be.

Musical by birth, the niggers were the first to create a march.

Slavery had long been abolished, and with it the meritocracy of the workforce. Affirmative action had permitted them access to occupations they had previously been excluded from. Reparations had been settled and guilt had been neatly laid upon the shoulders of white people everywhere, regardless if they ever even owned a slave in their lineage or even once, wisely, crossed a street after dark in a Harlem hood when a group of baggy clothed, red or blue bandana wearing, oversized tawdry jewellery exhibiting, untied sneakers tongue limp like a cows tongue, approached on the sidewalk ahead.

Everybody quickly upgraded their black and white television sets to techno-colour television sets so in not to appear racist. Other behaviours included owning at least one rhapsody compact disc, either TuPac or his rival, the rhapsody artist Notorious B.I.G., and if not these modern *artists*, one of the exploited niggers of the past, such as Louis Armstrong, or Ray Charles, or Stevland Hardaway Morris.

Because racism had long been eradicated in the country, it took a tremendous effort to undo the work of the great nigger, Martin Luther King Jr., who famously and with authority proclaimed that he "dreamed of a day where he would be judged on merit, and not the colour of his skin." Shortly after his martyrdom the world had come to judge everybody on merit—it was the era of all equality—but like the feminists and fags discovered, to be treated equally was difficult in that you had to become of value to society to be appreciated, thus desperately wished a return to the good old days of oppression, but only by using their self-proclaimed marginalization to oppress everybody who differed from themselves.

The work that undid the progress was first to take aim at police officers. The niggers always had an issue, incomprehensible to the majority population, of assaulting and murdering each other *en masse*. To this they were well versed in violence. Taking aim at police officers, inciting them to use force by aggressing the officers of the law at any chance they got, spitting at them, swearing, chest bumping, flashing nine's (which is nigger for handgun), threatening to rape and murder the officers family, encouraging their children to tote fake handguns to point at police officers of the law to have the officer draw their own service weapon in response; it was only a matter of time before a nigger got shot and when he did the ghettos banded together and exploded like a dam breaking over New Orleans. They marched and sold t-shirts and sang, Black Lives Matter! as if they hadn't since the progressive days of Martin Luther King Jr.. It is important to note that only the niggers could say, Black Lives Matter! White people had to say Nigger Lives Matter! so not to further the racist narrative.

Their march developed like this:

Inclusivity, Equality, the greatest Victim is me!

I'm Black and I'm under attack,

Destroy the White Supremacist Capitalistic Patriarchy!

And was first sung on all nigger radio stations, and Nigger Entertainment Television.

Finally, after several years of pretending to be oppressed and inciting incidents for attention to the cause, the Republic had back slid to a pre-MLK Jr. footing. The niggers even resurrected segregation in schools to keep white people from polluting the classroom.

The feminists and faggots owe much to the niggers for their work ethic. Soon, universities were returning to female only facilities, and the faggots were lobbying for their own schools, too. Though this became costly and eventually all parties settled for gender study courses, and faggot humanity studies, and nigger literature 101—most of which could be completed online or their degrees purchased in three easy payments of $19.99. The material confirmed their group oppression and proclaimed them all victims of the white patriarchy. Or something to that effect. Most certainly, these classes incubated the other marches.

The feminists decided upon:

Sexism is rampant here on my knees,

This feminist is fighting back!

Inclusivity, Equality, the greatest Victim is me!

And the faggots in rebuttal, though not in confrontation, coined their own verbiage to tack onto the feminists, who attached theirs to the nigger's.

The faggot march went like this:

Maybe that's true but what for LGTQB?

Sexual appetite deserves a plaque;

Down with the White Supremacist Capitalistic Patriarchy!

Needless to say, the Northern Republic was socialist by nature. And honestly come by to boot, as no one cared to read the Gulag Archipelago—understandably as it's three dense volumes—but at least one citizen, maybe their closet-faggot Prime Minister could have at least read the abridged version. Alas, he had not. No one had.

While all the men of the Republic, despised as they were, were deployed overseas to assist in the American initiative in keeping the invasion of sand-niggers from crossing the ocean, the closet-faggot Prime Minister passed a bill to change the Republic's anthem from the historic, "In all our Sons command," to the inclusive—albeit grammatically incorrect—"In all of Us command," and was ultimately dropped for the contemporary, Victim Villanelle. This was the Trojan Horse which began the fall of the Republic.

Everyone is familiar with Hilary Hamrod coining the phrase Islamophobic, which roughly translates to: a level-headed and often educated citizen holding reservations about a people who routinely throw faggots off roof tops, force their women into cloth bags, and pass death sentences on their own daughters after learning said daughters were gang raped by family friends and in offering themselves to be raped brought shame down upon the family.

Alas, despite warrant, the great and powerful Hilary manipulated the term Islamophobia to be insulting to the person to whom they labelled it. Namely, all free-thinking persons. The closet-faggot Prime Minister even made it law that if anyone was Islamophobic, they would be charged and imprisoned for up to five years.

To show absolute commitment to the idea, the closet-faggot Prime Minister awarded twelve-million dollars to a convicted Republic terrorist—who funnelled this money back into the training compounds of his terrorist sand-nigger family in the lands where the closet-faggot Prime Minister had deployed all Republic men to fight. It takes no historian to recognize the closet-faggot Prime Minister was funding the opposing army against his own countrymen. This was an extreme effort to eradicate all masculinity in the Republic.

Besides the closet-faggot Prime Minister changing the Republic's anthem and funding terrorism abroad, the closet-faggot Prime Minister also appointed a sand-nigger to head the Northern Republic Armed Forces. This orange turban wearing sand-nigger was not qualified at the time of appointment, however, because he refused to wear a regimental headdress and fought to wear his turban (though if this General would have ever seen combat, he would have worn a helmet instead of his flagrant orange towel) the closet-faggot Prime Minister applauded his initiative and gave him the position. The closet-faggot Prime Minister also permitted turban-wearing sand-niggers from the largely faggotted west coast to enter government (including a known terrorist if the Air India bombing from decades past—only none of the sensitive Northern Republic citizens understood history, and even the ones who did, believed in amnesty for their own victim-kin, what happened in the past stays in the past, we're the Northern Republic, they banded together. We accept everyone for who they are.

Soon the orange turban-wearing sand-nigger in charge of the Northern Republic Armed Forces, forced everybody in uniform to wear turbans so not to visibly discriminate from the two other turban-wearing sand-niggers already among the ranks of the brigade.

The Republic opened their borders to 250,000 sand-niggers annually, with the ambition to raise the entry number to 500,000 by the year 2021—fortunately the Great Fall occurred beforehand or these parasites may have converted all of Western Hemisphere. With the influx of sand-niggers, they were soon to coin their own march and join the ranks of the victim with the feminists, faggots, and rightful niggers, however, their chant began in their native tongue before they could translate it into oppressive English. It went:

Dur-durka durka durka durk durka dur-durka,

Durka durka, dur-durka, durk dur durka dur durka.

Dur-durka, Dur-durka, durk durka Durka dur durk!

Loosely translated:

Immigrants have rights and need guarantees,

Health care, education, and a place to relax.

Inclusivity, Equality, the greatest Victim is me!

Because of their inclusion, the Republic became the rape capital of the world, because the sand-nigger men formed gangs and raped all the white women who had not yet adopted burlap sacks and paper bags to cover themselves with.

The closet-faggot Prime Minister supported the sand-niggers in their conquest, chastising the white woman, if you do not embrace progress, you are enabling the White Supremacist Capitalistic Patriarchy, despite many of the woman having been nominal feminists before the parasite sand-niggers consumed the Republic. The raping finally ceased when all Republic women covered themselves with potato sacks and balaclavas, which proved warm in the harsh winter months, but otherwise restricted their movement, quality of life, and encouraged rampant pubic hair growth, which dreaded over their birthing canals and swelled under their armpits. But they are French and many were already accustomed to this unhygienic approach to grooming.

It's the same as when an institution offers benefits to entice people to become patrons or members, and in doing so, refuse to reward the already patrons or members of the organization. Take, for example, the modern banking system—modern in the sense of before the Great Fall. Banks earned their income from the amount of money they kept under management. To attract new customers, or clients, as they preferred to refer to the consumers as, banks often offered rewards for switching to their institution. Some banks offered free televisions when an account was opened. Some banks, notoriously southern, offered bolt-action rifles for new account owners. Often banks simply offered to match the first deposit into the account. This was great for bank-hoppers, but what for the customers who were already loyal to their bank? The reward was only available to new customers. The current and loyal customers got nothing.

This is how the teenage mothers of the Republic felt when the sand-niggers began receiving free healthcare and business grants and educational preference and social assistance and whatever else was afforded them because there were of a difference land—namely, the land of sand-niggers.

Not only teenage mothers, but single-mothers whores of all ages, as they all lived under the poverty line. This should not be a surprise, as graduation from the standard school system at the end of grade 12 is the single variable separating graduates who live above the poverty line and the failures who live below. This and a woman who at least finished the standard grade 12 level of schooling knew better than to allow a man to ejaculate in her birthing canal, hence social assistance and trailer parks and the statistical probability to be impoverished.

If this was only bad enough, but further to the poverty, the actions of these single-mother whores created its own poverty feedback loop. Undoubtedly hooked on pharmaceutical drugs or those of the illegal persuasion, they would not have the money to pay for said drugs and having already offered their birthing canal to be be ejaculated in for the selfish desire of owning a child that would always love them and never leave them as their repulsive and often borderline personalities caused those who once loved them to love them no longer—would again offer their birthing canals to be ejaculated into, to cover the expense of the drugs in the transference of the government subsidy, and subsequently give life to another welfare case. This was no problem as the Republic would provide for basic income and provisions, affording the now junkie single-mother whores the freedom to refrain from work, continue consuming drugs, and ultimately increase their output of degenerate children. It is a fact that most times involving these junkie single-mother whores—who for some perverted reasoning were touted as heroes among the Republic—because of the drug dealers she lay with, spread many of the known communicable diseases which came to infect 83.9% of the global population in the only recorded contemporary pandemic.

These parasites, native to the Republic, felt slighted by the sand-niggers receiving benefits over what they already weaseled, and realized they were being made the victim, too. They rose. They marched. They spread their legs to all who would become erect in their presence, and with much labour, they became the fifth recognized marginalized group of the Northern Republic, contributing nothing more except children who would grow up to follow in their whore mother's shadows and become the same sloths sunk into their La-Z-Boys purchased with Republic money in front of 64" LCD televisions bought with more Republic money.

Their chant was cleverly worded:

I've not finished school and I'm pregnant, can't you see?

I'm a product of this low-income pack;

It's the fucking White Supremacist Capitalistic Patriarchy!

And it was a home run—home run refers to the historic sport of baseball, a man's sport, which lost its relevance when the first and only movie which depicted the racist nature of the sport in exploiting the only black man who ever played, ran its four weeks in theatre but could no longer be leveraged to educate the public on how systemic the issue really was because the goal was to return to the pre-MLK Jr. days, and so the movie was outed as having lost its relevance in pursuit of progressive equality.

The march, which rose from the plight of the single-mother whores, catapulted them into the limelight. It even received special airtime each week, which marched between all marginalized artist who had their songs on the radio.

And now there were five. The feminists, the fags, the niggers, the sand-niggers, and the single-mothers whores (who represented poverty everywhere).

Of rational minded people, the ISIS becoming a protected group was the furthest from purview. The Islamic's were jacked up sand-niggers known for abusing women, persecuting those persons of different sexual appetites, for poor fashion, and so forth, contradicting what the other five groups stood united for. In fact, the estranged prophet, whose name can not be mentioned, meticulously presented the exploits of the ISIS in the docu-book *One Hundred Little Victories*. It is a disturbing publication.

The ISIS joining the ranks shouldn't have happened; but it did. And that through a sneaky loop-hole which only now in retrospect makes absolute sense. They were disliked, check, hated in some circles, check-check, and feared—and fear stems from being misunderstood—so thus, they were victims, too, of the White Supremacist Capitalistic Patriarchy. After Hilary Hamrod went on record calling the White Supremacist Capitalist Patriarchy the *ISISophobic*, the Republic determined that as a group, the ISIS met most of the victim conditions: They were largely from poor camel countries; they were not white, except for the single-mother whores who converted for the surplus of men willing to gang-bang them; and when the ISIS moved from their camel countries to the Republic, they were quite poor.

Since the ISIS were not known for their tolerance, in order to be elevated to marginalized status, they had to re-brand their dogma as the Religion of Peace. This caught on like wildfire. All of their attacks were viewed as natural reactions to the White Supremacist Capitalist Patriarchy and thus became justified. It very similar to how the SJW's supported ANTIFA, the masked thugs who performed gang attacks on unsuspecting whites—despite being white themselves, as niggers didn't attend rallies and wouldn't aim a can of mace in someones face when they could pull their nine and bust a cap instead.

The ISIS became the Religion of Love, and anybody who dared question their tactics and aggressive nature were immediately called ISISophobic and were stripped of their public standing and forfeited their jobs.

Still, the marginalized elite don't like religion, and many believed that to adhere to a religion there must be some mental deficiency or retardation in the believer, so in order for the ISIS to be added to the already five, they had to accept being categorized with all the other Retards and Cripples. The ISIS quickly accepted the terms. As soon as they were elevated to marginalized status, they killed all the Retards and Cripples—and were applauded for demonstrating such mercy. Many of the Zika-heads and Downsfolk, and Transgenders (when they were still labelled medically as suffering from gender dysphoria and lumped in with the retards), were quickly eradicated. The Transsexuals who survived the initial Mercy Campaign realized it was only a matter of time before they would receive mercy themselves and be dispatched like the other drools. They lobbied the faggots membership into their group instead. This became known as the mass-exodus from the ISIS, the only marginalized group to ever experience an exodus of such magnitude. The Retards and Cripples might have found refuge in another group, only they were retarded or lame and couldn't gather enough mental resources to access foresight—but mostly could not escape the mercy of the ISIS because they had no legs.

There march was created and sang like this:

Islam is about love, don't you dare disagree!

And what for being a paranoid insomniac?

Inclusivity, Equality, the greatest Victim is me!

Damn the White Supremacist Capitalistic Patriarchy!

The seven groups united and their marches were set to the tune of London Bridges Falling Down, because London falling is emblematic of the fall of the White Supremacist Capitalistic Patriarchy. Together, it sounded as:

Inclusivity, Equality, the greatest Victim is me!

I'm black and I'm under attack,

Destroy the White Supremacist Capitalistic Patriarchy!

Sexism is rampant here on my knees,

This feminist is fighting back!

Inclusivity, Equality, the greatest Victim is me!

Maybe that's true, but what for LGTQB?

Sexual preference deserves a plaque;

Down with the White Supremacist Capitalistic Patriarchy!

Immigrants have rights and need guarantees,

Health care, education, and a place to relax.

Inclusivity, Equality, the greatest Victim is me!

I've not finished school and I'm pregnant, can't you see?

I'm a product of this low-income pack;

It's the fucking White Supremacist Capitalistic Patriarchy!

Islam is about love, don't you dare disagree!

And what for being a paranoid insomniac?

Inclusivity, Equality, the greatest Victim is me!

Damn the White Supremacist Capitalistic Patriarchy!

With the Seven Marginalized officially codified, the prestige in being of the masses quickly diminished. Fortunately for the Republic, or so the Republic hoped, the fags presented intersectionality, based on their own already complicated group identity, and offered it as an overlay which could apply to all marginalized groups. A pointed system to determine exactly where one stood on the totem pole.

Something simple made complicated in desperation to save a system which glimpsed its own death. It used to be queers were queers. Or fags. And then they became capital "Q" Queer. During all their marches and bubble parties and unprotected bathroom stall sex, the designation was expanded to LGBT: Lesbian, Gay, Bisexual, and Transgender. They covered all their bases, although it seemed a little bit excessive. Lesbians are gay. Bisexual people are gay. Transgender people are gay. But everybody wants to be special, so it turned out Lesbians weren't gay.

Bisexual people weren't gay. Transgender people weren't gay. Something about sharing sexism as their common root of oppression.

Used to be nobody cared what you did behind closed doors, and everything was fine that way. Now everybody wanted to be defined by what they did behind closed doors, and not only that, but to have everybody praise them for it. So, all the weirdos came out of the woods, came out of the bathroom stalls, came out from the bed of truck drivers, and formed a line. To skim the complexity of the situation on hand, consider this condensed version of faggot identities.

Advocates were fags who actively worked to end intolerance while supporting social equity (whatever that meant); Allies were straight people who desperately wanted to be a fag but were not aroused by the same sex and so they could only support queer and transfolk; the Androgyny-ites were fags who expressed themselves with elements of both masculinity and femininity; Asexuals, like the eunuchs of old, were fags who generally did not experience sexual attraction to any group of people; Bisexuals were fags who had an emotional, romantic, or sexual attraction for a person of more than one gender; Closeted fags—consider the closet-faggot Prime Minister of the Republic—were fags who keep their sexuality or gender identity a secret and had yet to come out of the closet; Cross-dressers were fags who got off from dressing in the clothing of the opposite gender; Fluid fags were fags who fluctuated between all the options; Gays and Lesbians were fags who had an emotional, romantic, or sexual attraction for people of the same sex; Intersex were fags who identified with dragons and cats and turtles and such; Pansexuals were fags who experience sexual, romantic, physical, and spiritual attraction for everybody inside the fag identity group, excluding white male hetero, as they were the patriarchy and the cause of all oppression; Queer used to be used to defy sexual restrictions, but under the regime became an expletive—kind of like how the savages alternated between Indian and Native Peoples, dependent on whichever term their oppressor used they could insist on the other and further show how the oppressor continued in their tyranny; the Questioning were fags who wanted to get their feet wet but were afraid of the water; Same Gender Loving or SGL's were what the niggers used as an alternative to gay and lesbian so to separate them from the white fag community; Stealth's were fags who lived their self-identified genders without other people knowing that they were transsexual fags (but everybody always knew); Transsexuals were fags whose self-identified gender did not match society's expectations of someone with their sex characteristics; and finally Two-Spirited were savage fags who had both masculine and feminine spirits.

The one group of sexual deviants they didn't accept were the pedophiles. Initially, it was not considered kosher to lust over the delicate, virgin, petite, glowing body of a child. About a year after the ISIS joined with the Retards and Cripples to complete the group of seven, the pedophiles were acknowledged as Allies under the faggot umbrella—because to suck dick or eat cunt against traditional biological programming is not a choice. Paedophilia, therefor, shouldn't be a crime as it's their natural inclination to prefer children and this feature should instead be celebrated. Each group identity contained its own intersectionality and corresponding hierarchical position. For example, the traditional pedophile is similar to the heterosexual white male. He's plain. There are, however, Fluid Pedophiles, much more respected among the fag populace, who fluctuated between the mix of options available: man and woman, gay and straight, Ze, Hir, and etc.. And this yet without defining their sexual appetites, e.g. attraction to male identities under the age of four. It was a beautiful display of all deviants propping each other up.

These were most of the unique identities within the LGBT species, and although they were lumped together here as being identical to each other; they insisted that there were specific needs and concerns related to each individual identity, and so quarterly, the Brahman of each identifier and Brahmans of other identity groups not yet included in the

L.G.B.T.Q.I.A.+ acronym, met to discuss the merits of affording other groups protection under the equality umbrella. Brahmans from the Dragonflies, the Aliens, the Mushrooms, the Fetuses, the Electronics, the Infants, the Tri-Androgynies and the Asexual-Bigenders attended each quarterly mass.

This was the atmosphere to which the men decided the kids had played long enough. With no public recourse available, the straight white men gathered together, stripped, and engaged in faggot coitus. This was not for enlightenment. These men were not gay. They did not enjoy corn-holing, or the smell of shit on their partially slumped penises. Many of the men gagged and vomited, and on first penetration exploded feces all over their partners. No. If any of these brave men were here today, they would confirm, the orgy of men, legion, were simply doing what had to be done. Because that's what real men did.

See, these men, these peasant caste white heterosexual males, remembered what the world had forgotten.

Faggot anal coitus spread the acquired immunodeficiency syndrome—and that shit kills.

You could see it on the withering faces of the L.G.B.T.Q.I.A.+ everywhere. The slow death. The cigarette burned eyes. The pale skin, unless hidden beneath the orange-tinted skin from the artificial UV— another sentence of nature's justice in correcting wayward humanity. You could see it in their thin faces, unless plumped from Botox—it seemed the louder they proclaimed their happiness, their actions focused on their lust for death. They evidenced it in their diet pills and unregulated supplements. A race to the grave—and to take everybody with.

Except for the men. The men knew death claimed soon enough. Better to get up in the morning, do their work, eat their dinner, rest a while, and retire to sleep. It wasn't much. But it was something. Only not anymore. Despite the endless attempts to destroy masculinity, men never stopped being men. They got up, worked, went to bed and kept the world turning. And so, these men, doing what they always did, seeing the issue for what it was, then determining to fix it, they stripped down to their birthday suits and fucked like they were fucking their once appreciative wives. Semen entered assholes at a rate never even tried at a Pulse nightclub. Blood dripped down legs. The pungent, sour-hinted sweet aroma of various feces consistency thickened the air. The saltine tears which threatened to singe the cheeks of these brave soldiers were quickly wiped away while they dressed. It was D-Day all over again. A suicide mission. But necessary for survival.

The men returned home and continued their routines, getting up, working, going to bed. They rarely saw their wives anymore. The women were always moving about, busy, but never having much to show for it, and often only returning late in the evening, or in the early morning hours.

It was their right to be sexually liberated, dammit!

It was their right to murder unborn children if they wanted.

That's what being liberated meant. Doing whatever you wanted whenever you wanted. Men, on the other hand, understood autonomy to be the ability to lead disciplined lives.

As a power move, wives withheld sex from their husbands, and in the off chance when they were hot and bothered and fired up to fuck they'd demand a go at pegging. Pegging was penis envy.

Woman wore special jockstraps designed to fit plus sizes which had a overlapped slit at the crotch like a man's pair of boxer shorts. Through this slit they would slide a silicon baton to simulate a man's throbbing penis. Though they were available in flesh tones, the women, exercising their liberation, preferred colours of purple and pink and cherry red. Until then, the men had resisted these rape-fantasy advances. But not anymore. This time they were ready. They could feel it in their veins. The AIDS, slowly commanding control of their bodies. Yes. Now, it was time.

When the wives strapped up and slapped their faux-penises on the table where their husbands were eating a solemn last meal, they were prepared, because men are always prepared. They negotiated. If I do this for you, I want to finish how we used to (as in ejaculating into the birthing canal).

Overzealous at their apparent victory, the women most hurriedly accepted the counteroffer.

And so it began.

There was less blood this time around, as the men had already stretched their assholes once. Some even ejaculated prematurely from the stimulation to the prostate. This hadn't been accounted for. Still, enough men endured like warriors, and when their wives were satisfied with the pegging, the men mounted them and exploded tainted jism into their birthing canals.

Soon, and in part because all the liberated fags had already been carrying and spreading the virus, 99.999999999999999% of the world population was HIV+ and died a little quicker each day.

Only a select populous of vegetarian Jaines who had moved to the coniferous north of the Republic at the turn of the century, remained unscathed of all the crockery spread about the world. They carried on with disinterested concern, treading lightly and purposing to do no harm, while the rest of the world died.

www.ingramcontent.com/pod-product-compliance
Lightning Source LLC
Chambersburg PA
CBHW031351160726
47993CB00002B/919